THE EXISTENTIAL ACTOR
LIFE AND DEATH, ONSTAGE AND OFF

THE EXISTENTIAL ACTOR
LIFE AND DEATH, ONSTAGE AND OFF

JEFF ZINN

SMITH AND KRAUS 2015

Library of Congress Control Number: 2015941856
ISBN: 978-57525-9000

Typesetting, layout, and cover design by Olivia Monteleone

Cover photo: Robert Kropf in *Love Song* by John Kolvenbach
Back cover photo: Jeff Zinn by Susan Wilson

A Smith and Kraus book
177 Lyme Road, Hanover, NH 03755
editorial 603.643.6431 To Order 1.877.668.8680
www.smithandkraus.com

To Crystal

ACKNOWLEDGMENTS

I owe a debt of gratitude, first and foremost, to Professor Sheldon Solomon, whose work on Terror Management Theory first alerted me to Ernest Becker and the possibility of connecting his ideas to the theater. Sheldon has graciously allowed me to repurpose several of his constructs, including "The three questions." Thanks also to Neil Elgee and the Ernest Becker Foundation for their support and encouragement. I want to thank my theater mentors, Ronald Bennett, Robert Brustein, Susan Batson, and Patsy Rodenburg. Robert Scanlan introduced me to action and the four causes of Aristotle. Robert J. Lifton was most generous with his time, and our conversations expanded my understanding of psychology.

I had the benefit of a number of people who read early drafts and responded generously with their notes and comments: Brendan Hughes, Florence Philips, Michael Klein, Ellie Rubin, Jeffrey Sweet, Tom Kee, Stephen Russell, and especially Brenda Withers, David Strathairn and Todd London. My great thanks to Stef Stendardo who copy-edited multiple drafts. Thanks also to my editor Jayne Benjulian who helped me bring the manuscript into its finished form.

Of course, I must thank my parents, Roslyn and Howard Zinn, who always encouraged me in my life in the theater. My wife, Crystal, has been my chief sounding board, functioning somehow as both fierce critic and unconditional supporter. I thank her for her love and patience in seeing me through what must have seemed a never ending project.

A Note on Sources

Rather than pepper the manuscript with footnotes, I have chosen to include a bibliography in the back pages of the book.

The author would like to thank Carol Rocamora for the use of her translations in *Chekhov: Four Plays*, and *Ivanov*, and Rick Davis and the late, Brian Johnston, for their translations in *Ibsen: Four Major Plays*.

All other quotations are taken under the fair use provision of international copyright law.

TABLE OF CONTENTS

FOREWORD

The actor's life is one epiphany after another. That's what happens when you attune your sensitivities to human emotion and behavior, to the personal and interpersonal. That's what happens when you search for the truth of how we live. You make discoveries, large and small explosions of insight. Revelations burst forth, even when it might look to the rest of us as though you're just learning lines.

For actors, these discoveries often begin in the body – throat, diaphragm, muscle, the geography of tension and ease, the places feelings lodge and from which they emanate. Physical awareness leads to connection. First, breath connects you to spirit (they even share an etymology, along with inspiration). Then your voice reaches another's ear. Your muscles allow you to approach and touch. Through it all, feeling radiates, tying actor to audience in ways that, in the theatre, remain as mysterious as they are powerful.

It's a mistake, though, to view the epiphanies of acting romantically. Theatre is a passionate art, but it's also an intellectual one. It marries the emotional and philosophical, the visceral and literary. Theatre persists, despite centuries of death proclamations, because it is, as the New Agers like to say, holistic. The discoveries actors make have to be holistic, too, or they roll away like beads spilled on a floor. Beads (or, in the actor's lingo, beats, the small units of action that make up a scene) need thread. Discoveries need to add up to qualify as truth.

What if there were a way to tie these acting discoveries together? What if there were a master theory of acting, a grand unified theory, the sort that physicists seek to explain the universe?

What if, as Jeff Zinn wonders in the book you are about to read, there were, for actor training and performance, a "theory of everything"? I can't guarantee you that Zinn has found everything, but he's onto something big.

Chances are – if you act, direct, write or design for the theatre, or if you are learning how – "theory" makes you wary. We are practical people, theatre folk. We seek concrete behavior to illuminate all that is invisible between us in this world. Will a master theory help you create a character? Will Existentialist Philosophy solve the problems of a scene? Can understanding how we spend our days in denial of death give performance life?

Stop for a minute, though. What if you had the chance to understand how all the wildly disparate and maybe mutually exclusive "schools" of acting fit together? What if you could gather together centuries of actor training and performance style in a way that made helpful sense now? What if all those approaches – and with them all those gnarly terms like action, intention, imagination, subtext, style, super-objective, psychological gesture, viewpoints, Method – what if they all could be boiled down to a mere four categories, a grid both comprehensible and profound? More, what if this road to understanding the art of acting was actually a way to understand our humanity. (It is a grand theory after all.)

I've always found acting the most natural metaphor for being human. Acting requires presence. It requires empathy, sensory awareness, and mental focus. Acting is, as has often been noted, listening. It calls for give-and-take, emotional access, sharing space and time with others. Acting, like life, means making scenes, wanting more, pushing through conflict, loving, hating, fighting, conquering, failing, and falling. We act as we live – in relationship, in society, and on the clock.

We are always, theatre reminds us, on the clock. Theatre intensifies the reality that, as Shakespeare famously wrote, "Life is but . . . a poor player that struts and frets his hour upon the stage." An hour is all we get. In *The Existential Actor*, Jeff Zinn heightens our awareness of this hour, the being that goes with human. He subtitles the work, *Life and Death, Onstage and Off.* We exist, therefore we act. Our acting becomes a way of living with the knowledge that our existence is timed.

This is a book for the thinking actor, and the finest actors I've known are just that. The best actors bring it all together – body, heart, spirit, and mind. This book is for the actor who thinks about craft and influence, who thinks about the relationship of performance to living, who thinks about *doing* and what that doing means. Acting is a metaphor and it's a mirror, and, so, a theory of acting, if true, shows us to ourselves.

Jeff Zinn knows this. He knows it as an actor, director, teacher, and thinker. His "theory of everything" is simple and revelatory. In order to portray life, you have to understand how tenuously we grasp it, how carefully we construct the stories of our own heroism, how ferociously we defend them. Character, and by extension characters, emerge from these self-stories and from the behavior with which they are defended. When characters converge and the narratives they hold most dear collide, you've got a play. The stakes are always the same. That's the thing about stories, as Zinn helps us see with glaring clarity: they are always a matter of life and death.

—Todd London
April, 2015

13

FOUR ELEMENTS: A NEW THEORY FOR THE THEATER

When we go to the theater we want what happens onstage to be a matter of life and death. Some will argue that this is wrong: that what we want most of all is to be entertained, to be taken OUT of the realm of our day-to-day existences and transported to some other, better, or at least, more aesthetically pleasing place. But I would argue that, despite what we may think we want from our entertainments, what we really need – and by that I mean the theatrical experience that best entertains us – is actually the one in which the stakes are enormously high; a matter of life and death, in fact. When those stakes are not sufficiently high, we often lose interest. We change the channel.

Theater makers know this intuitively. As directors we implore actors to raise the stakes. As actors we search for deep connections to our characters, making their concerns our concerns, trying hard to generate a sense of heightened importance. Often we find ourselves employing the language of analogy and metaphor. We use the technique of *substitution*; swapping out the actor standing right in front of us for an imaginary other – a parent, a lover – so that we might believe more fully in what we're doing. We employ the *magic if* made famous by Stanislavski: *what if* I were the prince of Denmark? *What if* I were a high school science teacher dying of cancer who goes into the meth trade?

Exercises that stimulate the imagination can help us find pathways into a character, but they also reinforce the notion that the characters we portray are *other*, fundamentally different from ourselves, and portraying them requires some kind of technical bridge. But aren't the most elemental fears, needs, and motivations of our characters also our most elemental fears, needs, and motivations? This book explores how we might begin to deepen that understanding and so bring a sense of life-and-death urgency to everything we create or interpret.

A little more than 20 years ago I made a discovery that changed my approach to theater. For almost 20 years before that, first as an actor, then as a director, I had been obsessed with the question of how we do this acting thing. How can we do it well? How can we do it better? Like so many young actors, I read the great books by the master teachers: Stanislavski, Sandy Meisner, Bobby Lewis, Stella Adler, and Uta Hagen, and even studied with a few of them. I also attended the performances and delved into the writings of the more experimental wing of the American and world theater: Peter Brook, Richard Foreman, Jerzy Grotowski, Antonin Artaud, Mabou Mines, and others. I performed on, off, and off-off Broadway and toured with improvisational comedy companies. I directed at the West Bank Café, Ensemble Studio Theatre, the Circle Rep Lab and at regional theaters around the country. Eventually I landed at Wellfleet Harbor Actors Theater where I served as artistic director for 25 years. Processing all these influences and experiences, and working with actors who themselves had trained in various schools and disciplines, I began to notice four big ideas cropping up in various forms and in various combinations. They go by different names, but I have come to call them *shape, action, transaction,* and *surrender.*

The most ancient traditions, and what we think of as more conventional, so-called "classical" approaches, have relied mostly on *shape*: the external, physical manifestations of character. Contemporary schools and techniques have added other elements: the Actors Studio, for instance, has always focused on the authentic expression of emotion – what I call *surrender.* Teachers at The Neighborhood Playhouse, with their emphasis on deep listening and reliance on the repetition exercise, have made *transaction* the focus. Across a wide array of schools and disciplines we find reference to motivation and intention, and choosing *actions* that might accomplish those objectives. It is also impossible not to notice that the many schools and camps, relying on one or more of these elements, are often in conflict with one another. A classical actor might be dismissive of Stanislavski; the Neighborhood Playhouse people challenge the acolytes of the Actors Studio, and vice versa. Everyone puts down Broadway. So I got very excited when I stumbled on a set of ideas that seemed to offer the possibility of tying it all together. They came, not from the world of theater, but rather from philosophy and psychology, which routinely asks questions about what motivates human behavior.

My eureka moment came while, as a grad student at the ART Institute, I was directing *The Killer*, one of Eugene Ionesco's more difficult (and rarely produced) plays. The main character, Berenger, is an ordinary man living a banal life. One day he takes the wrong train and finds a hidden "radiant city." He is met by the Architect of the city who welcomes him warmly and shows him around. It's an amazing place, everything the world Berenger left behind is not: clean, spacious, filled with light and air and friendly people. A charming young woman appears, Dany, the Architect's assistant. Berenger is instantly smitten and declares that they are engaged. But then things begin to turn sour. We hear the sound of breaking glass and a muffled scream. The Architect reluctantly discloses that there is a problem in the radiant city: a killer is at large, striking randomly and without cause. Berenger's initial feelings of euphoria are replaced by dread:

...Oh dear, and I'd already felt I'd taken hold in these surroundings! Now all the brilliance they offer is dead.... I can feel the darkness spreading inside me again! ... I feel shattered, stunned... My tiredness has come on again... There's no point in living! What's the good of it all, what's the good if it only brings us to this? Stop it, you must stop it Superintendent.

Another scream is heard. Word arrives: Dany is dead. Horrified, grief stricken, Berenger is infused with purpose. He embarks on a mission to avenge Dany's death. But the inhabitants of the radiant city are strangely apathetic and want Berenger to abandon his quest. The killer has always been there. Leave it alone.

Berenger reminded me of Bernhard Goetz, the New York City straphanger so afraid of being mugged that he shot several would-be assailants in self-defense – or so he claimed. The core of the play seemed to be Berenger's misplaced attempt to personify the evil that was in society. If he could only identify, locate, and punish the killer, the radiant city would become a safe place for good people to live. A perfectly reasonable analysis. Then it hit me that what Berenger feared most was not just a killer but his own mortality. His true nemesis was the fact of death itself.

It was at this point that I serendipitously came upon a New York Science Times article by Daniel Goleman describing a series of experiments testing the late Ernest Becker's "sweeping theory that gives the fear of death a central and often unsuspected role in psychological life." In his 1974 Pulitzer Prize winning book, *The Denial of Death*, Becker argued that cultural worldviews exist primarily to buffer us from awareness of death. Those deep attachments that we have to nations, political parties, ethnic identities, and even sports teams, function primarily to buffer us from awareness of death. This goes a long way to explain why, when those worldviews are challenged, we are moved to defend them so fiercely, even to the point of annihilating the "other."

This notion, that worldview protects us from the fear of death, was the working hypothesis being tested by experimental social psychologist Sheldon Solomon and his colleagues. In their study entitled, *Tales From The Crypt: On The Role Of Death In Life*, published in *Zygon: Journal of Religion and Science,* they recounted how:

> *... we developed a simple paradigm in which people are asked to think about their own death—what we will henceforth refer to as* mortality salience—*and then to make judgments about others who either violate or uphold important aspects of their cultural worldviews.*

A group of 22 municipal court judges in Tucson Arizona who volunteered for the study were given questionnaires in which half of them were asked to write a short essay describing their feelings surrounding their own deaths; "what you think will happen to you as you physically die and once you are physically dead." The other half of the judges served as the control group and were not given this questionnaire. According to the Times article:

> *The judges were then asked to set bond for a prostitute based on a case brief describing the circumstances of her arrest. Those who did not reflect on death before setting the bond recommended, on average, that it be $50. But the average bond was $455 among those who had been thinking about their own death.*

That's a factor of almost ten to one. I hurried to my local bookstore (this is pre-Amazon) to locate a copy of *The Denial of Death.* In its opening paragraph I read:

The idea of death, the fear of it, haunts the human animal like nothing else; it is a main-spring of human activity–activity designed largely to avoid the fatality of death, to overcome it by denying in some way that it is the final destiny for man.

Becker goes on to argue that the fear of death coupled with a fear of life – overwhelming when perceived in its fullness – demands that we devise coping strategies for both denying our mortality and narrowing down the immensity of life. These strategies manifest in what he called the *causa sui project;* an identity that each person adopts or creates in order to feel that life is purposeful. Without the *causa sui* (the cause of oneself) we have only the raw truth of existence: the universe is infinitely more powerful, beautiful, and meaningful than we are, and, furthermore, we will soon die. The *causa sui* is a vital lie that we construct to provide some illusion of purpose in a random and oblivious universe.

My head exploded.

In the theater we are constantly interrogating the intentions of our characters. "What's my motivation?" – an eye-roll-inducing cliché – is also a real question that must be asked and answered each time we create or interpret the actions of a character. If, as Becker suggested, awareness and fear of mortality are the bottom layer in the sediment of human motivation, theater makers

Ernest Becker

might mine that awareness and allow it to function more consciously in our process. Here's how we might begin to connect the dots:

- Throughout our lives we are in the process of creating and inhabiting an identity that takes a specific **shape** heavily influenced by the culture we inhabit. This self-created identity, our *causa sui* project, takes the form of a heroic narrative, the story we tell ourselves and others about who we are. The narrative is *heroic* because, like the mythic heroes whose deeds outlive them, it provides us with a sense of symbolic immortality, shielding us from the paralyzing fact of death. In theatrical terms, *shape* embodies "outside-in" approaches both historical and contemporary in its emphasis on costume, language, period, and gesture. It's how we dance and move, what we drive, what we wear, and what we believe. It is what we look like on the outside, but it's also how we see ourselves on the inside.

- **Action** is what we *do* after we figure out what we want. Motivation, intention, objective, all of these common theatrical terms come together when we decide on and execute an *action*. Once we establish the importance of the identity defining, death-denying *shape* we have assumed, its construction and defense can be understood to be the underpinning of every *action* that we take, onstage and off.

- **Transactions** with other people are our means of knowing when we've accomplished our *action*. It is essential to our sense of well-being that the actions we take are reinforced and validated in the *transactions* we enter into with the people with whom we come into contact both onstage and off. We find this element emphasized in the repetition exercises of Sanford Meisner and in the *second circle* of Patsy Rodenburg.

- When events cause identity to break down and the psychological armor can no longer shield us from our mortality – our vulnerability – the deep emotions we have been holding back are released in an act of **surrender**. *Surrender* is what we feel and how we allow ourselves to feel. Authentic emotional release is the holy grail for many theatrical techniques, especially those preached by Lee Strasberg and others who continued along the path paved by Stanislavski. It has also been central to the work of postmodernists such as Jerzy Grotowski and Lee Breuer. Surrender arrives when the primary action of constructing an identity fails, when the shape shatters and we peel away the psychological armor that shape provides.

What happens onstage must be a matter of life and death because everything we do in life, every action that we take, is in support of the *heroic narrative*, the story of ourselves that imbues our actions with a sense of meaning, purpose, and, yes, immortality. The notion that fictional characters and real people share this fundamental mechanism of motivation and self-creation is at the center of everything I will be talking about in these pages.

This is a book about acting but it is also about human beings in life and in literature. It includes a historical survey of approaches to the art and craft of acting, but it also offers my own synthesis of those many approaches, grounded in some very powerful ideas drawn from philosophy, psychology, social science, and even theology. Part of the reason it has taken me so long to bring this project to fruition is because I have struggled to arrive at the proper sequence to present these disparate concepts. Should I begin with the psychology and risk losing the theater audience which is, after all, its main target? Or should I dive right into the history of acting theories? Ultimately I decided to begin with the larger philosophical and psychological concepts because, without that foundation, what follows would not make much sense. In Part Two I survey the myriad approaches to the art and craft of the actor, from Aristotle to Stanislavski and beyond. Some approaches have generated large catalogues of important elements – Stanislavski's "system" has about 40 – others are quite narrowly focused and resolve to only one or two elements. In Part Three I offer my own broad theory for the theater, a synthesis drawn from these many approaches, in four stand-alone chapters that explore, in some depth, the four elements: *shape, action, transaction,* and *surrender.*

Part Four tests a number of plays, spanning a range of

genres and periods, against these ideas. If *The Existential Actor* coheres as a broad theory for the theater, it should help us make sense of any plays we might approach.

For now, I offer the following thumbnail by way of example:

In *Death of a Salesman,* Willy Loman's *shape* is that of the all-American super-salesman. His entire sense of himself as a heroic figure is bound up in that identity. Every *action* he takes in the course of the play is in the service of defending that life choice. The rightness of that shape, the success or failure of his actions, is reflected back to him in the *transactions* he has with his wife, his sons, his boss, his brother, his neighbor. As the failure of his choices becomes clear, the psychological armor he has built up all his life begins to crumble, and there is an emotional release – a *surrender* – that variously takes the form of anger, tears, manic laughter, and disorientation. The actors portraying Willy, Biff, Linda – indeed any of the play's characters – might begin the process of creating a character and building a role by first exploring their own *causa sui* project.

I have chosen the four elements, *shape, action, transaction,* and *surrender,* with care because, while each of them is central to the psychological mechanisms of character creation, each one also embodies core principles that have been explored and utilized by theater theorists and practitioners as diverse as Aristotle, Grotowski, Stanislavski, Brecht, Strasberg, and Meisner.

But the four elements are not intended to be solely a bundle of techniques for actors. They also function as a dramaturgical lens through which anyone interested in exploring and understanding character – writers, directors, readers, lovers of theater – can observe with a fresh perspective how character is formed in the first place and how those creatures of the imagination might be created or interpreted.

PART I

Life and Death

ONE

MORTALITY SALIENCE –
AWARENESS OF DEATH

One of the things that make us human is that we know we're alive. We're absolutely conscious of the fact that we exist. This awareness is literally awesome, exhilarating, and potentially joyous. But as Adam and Eve learned the hard way, knowledge is a bitter fruit. Cast out of Eden, their initial euphoria and sense of themselves as godlike creations of God is replaced by the understanding that they are nothing more than animals, or as experimental social psychologist Sheldon Solomon has put it, "…breathing, defecating, urinating, vomiting, expectorating, perspiring, menstruating, ejaculating, exfoliating, postnasal dripping, pieces of meat, no more significant or enduring than cockroaches or cucumbers."

It was Kierkegaard who first used the Eden myth to capture this tension in our natures. He observed that if we were either completely of the spirit or completely animal we might live in blissful innocence. But because we are aware of our dual status as "godlike" creatures, we experience both joy and dread. The word Kierkegaard used – *angst* – is usually understood as "anxiety," but a more accurate translation includes feelings of both anxi-

Søren Kierkegaard

ety and exaltation. Simply being alive and fully feeling that aliveness can induce feelings of ecstasy, but as the temporary nature of our existence becomes salient a sense of dread creeps in behind the exaltation.

Exactly when does the awful knowledge of our mortality assert itself? It's there in the cry of the baby – feed me, hold me, love me, or I'll die. Then, if we're lucky and have someone who will feed us, hold us, love us, and protect us from whatever is awful, we are able to live awhile in the safe cocoon of young childhood. Eventually, though, we start asking and we are told: "Yes, things die. People die. Parents die. YOU will die, but not for a long, long time...." Except that it's a lie. The hard truth about death is that it really can and does come at any time. So we lie. We lie to our children as we teach our children not to lie.

That we will not die is the vital lie that all cultures construct for themselves. It's at the center of huge edifices of belief and worldview that we inherit and in which we participate all our lives. These belief systems help us feel that we are not so vulnerable, not quite so mortal. They help us feel that we are at least symbolically, if not literally, immortal. We construct these lies because the angst named by Kierkegaard is too intense for us to carry around in every moment.

No matter how well constructed the lies, there are times when the full awareness of our impossible status as mortal gods comes crashing down upon us. This awareness may intrude at times that are unexpected and unwelcome. There are also times when we deliberately seek it out. (More on that later.) What does this have to do with the theater? Plenty. We go to the theater, we go to the movies, we read novels and watch TV, we tell stories and listen to stories because we are, all of us, insatiably curious about *us*. We want to understand why we do what we do. We identify with characters. They are like us and they are not like us. They get into jams and they get out of jams.

When we go to the theater we prefer the stakes onstage to be life and death even when the circumstances appear to be relatively low key. Why? Because if they're not we lose interest. We turn away. Our own lives mostly lack drama, which is to say that the life-and-death struggle lurking in the background has been put safely out of view. Theater is most effective when it brings back into view that which we have conveniently blocked out; the inevitability of death. The theater is a place where we can temporarily break through the buffers and engage these hardest of truths head-on.

In the real world, death awareness can elicit a kind of stage fright. What if you believed – not just intellectually, but viscerally – that right outside your door the chances were even that a sniper would fire at you from a hidden vantage point, a car would run you down, a passing meteor would veer off course and smash into the earth, annihilating not just you but all of life? The result would be paralysis. Catatonia and agoraphobia are only the most extreme forms of stage fright, a sense of being frozen in the wings, that sometimes renders us unable to step out onto the stages of our lives. Events like 9/11 and the Boston Marathon bombings remind us that these fears are grounded in reality and only reinforce how vulnerable we are.

Woody Allen successfully mined this to great comic effect in the film *Annie Hall* when the young Alvy Singer is taken to a psychiatrist by his mother:

> *Mother: He's been depressed. All of a sudden he can't do anything!*
> *Psychiatrist: Why are you depressed, Alvy?*
> *Alvy: The universe is expanding.*
> *Psychiatrist: The universe is expanding?*
> *Alvy: Well, the universe is everything, and if it's expanding, someday it will break apart, and that will be the end of everything.*
> *Mother: What is that your business? He's stopped doing his homework!*
> *Alvy: What's the point?*

The solution, according to Ernest Becker and others, is to wrap ourselves in layers of psychological armor. *Culture* provides that armor: a ready-made framework, a worldview complete with rules for how to walk, talk, dress, and behave. Biological factors are determinative, of course, and none of us chooses our parents or the complicated stew of genes and chromosomes that shape us. But once we have drawn the lottery ticket that is handed out at birth, culture takes over with that "set of beliefs about the nature of reality people share in groups." It is culture that reduces anxiety associated with the awareness of death by accomplishing two important functions: First, it lends meaning by providing us with answers to universal cosmological questions about the nature of life – answers that reassure us that the world we live in is a stable, orderly, meaningful place. Second, it allows us to feel that we ourselves are valuable people who play significant roles in that universe.

We can imagine how these culturally devised solutions might have begun: Casting ourselves back in time to the earliest moments of self-aware humanity we can picture our ancestors tenuously perched in a rugged and inhospitable environment, gazing at the stars and confronting the mysteries of their universe. It must have been discombobulating to exist in a harsh terrain confronted by the fact of a natural world capable of dispensing incredible bounty, but also utter devastation and sudden death. They must have wondered:

Where do we come from?

What are we supposed to do while we're here?

Where do we go after we die?

THE 3 BIG QUESTIONS,
PAUL GAUGUIN

Today we may congratulate ourselves for knowing so much more than they did, for having so many answers whose truths would have been inconceivable to their primitive brains. Yet the answers to those basic questions allowed our forebears to feel that the universe was an orderly place with rules for living. Observing those rules conferred meaning and acceptance. The questions still resonate because the answers devised by cultures are, even today, works in progress. Contemporary philosophers and psychologists still grapple with them. Martin Heidegger famously rephrased the first question as, "Why are there beings at all instead of just nothing?"

We don't come up with answers to the three questions on our own. In fact, we don't really come up with anything on our own. We know that infants are aware of others even before they are aware of themselves. The construction of the human self is something that happens from the outside in. We only know what we know about ourselves because of what we receive from the outside world. This simple idea of validation from others will take on huge importance when we start to explore *transaction*.

The Three Questions

Every culture answers the first question, "where do we come from?" in its own way. Perhaps with, "In the beginning God created the heavens and the earth...." A quick Google of "creation myths," however, returns a long list of fabulous tales from the Babylonian to the Yoruba:

CREATION OF ADAM

- The Boshongo, a Bantu tribe, believe that "in the beginning, Bumba was all alone in the water. Then he got sick and vomited the sun, moon, stars and land...."

- The Yokut believe that life on earth began with a great flood, "...then out of the sky one day glided an enormous eagle with a black crow riding upon its back, searching for a place to light...."
- Greek myth begins with Chaos ruled by the goddess Eurynome. She mates with the wind to produce Earth and Sky who themselves mate to create a race of Titans led by Cronus.

You and I may find these stories amusing. But who's to say that one worldview – ours – is true and the others false? Does it even matter? Sheldon Solomon suggests:

> *Culture really has nothing to do with the truth. If anything, its function is to obscure the horrifying possibility that we live in a random and indeterminate universe in which the only certain outcome is death and destruction.*

The answers to the second question, "What do we do while we're here?" are too numerous to be contained in a simple story told by the fire or in the opening chapter of a Bible. Those answers require libraries, museums, and educational, legal, and political institutions. They reside in endless catalogs of science, art, and law. Each culture generates its own versions of these things and communicates them to its members in a million ways: parent to child, peer to peer, through educational systems, and through the media. Thousands of years before the birth of Christ, oral histories handed down through generations of

Sheldon Solomon

lyric poets found their way into some of the first written narratives of western culture. *The Iliad* and *The Odyssey* spelled out intricate codes of conduct; ways of being in the world. Buried inside those fabulous tales was almost everything one might need to know about how to behave in the realms of love, war, property, marriage, friendship, loyalty, generosity, how to grieve death properly, and what constitutes heroism.

Within each culture exist subcultures that include separate religions, nations, political parties, "isms," sports teams, and professions, each with their own rules and regulations, jargon, dress, and codes of behavior. All of them provide the individual with a blueprint for answering question number two; the question of what we are to do while we're here and even *how* we are to do it. Adherence to the code of any culture or subculture helps define success and failure and provides an essential sense of self-worth. These culturally determined codes of behavior, which include how we dress, how we dance, the languages we speak, the dialects and regional accents within those languages, are what go into the broad category I call *shape*.

In chapter 13 I will explore the notion of *shape* in some depth. For now, I want to reiterate that the experiments conducted by Sheldon Solomon and many others have helped to demonstrate how strongly we are attached, and how deeply our behavior is affected, by adherence to these worldviews. In addition to the experiment I cited earlier in which judges, after contemplating their mortality, rendered especially harsh sentences on prostitutes, over 300 empirical studies have been published attesting to the validity and power of the *mortality salience effect*.

The third question, "What happens to us after we die?" goes to the very heart of this business of immortality. Society confers either literal or symbolic immortality upon those members who conform to and abide by the roles and rules of those cultures. Literal immortality is promised by various religions, with different versions of life after death. We may be tempted to relegate this notion of *literal* immortality to primitive and/or prehistoric cultures until we consider that

74% of all Americans believe in an afterlife. And it is not just a matter of personal belief. The constitutions of seven states still contain articles that prohibit nonbelievers from holding public office. North Carolina spells it out: "The following persons shall be disqualified for office: First, any person who shall deny the being of Almighty God."

Literal belief in life after death requires "faith." Symbolic immortality, however, is available to all and can be acquired through the works we do, especially creative works, that remain after we are gone. Builders of pyramids, bridges, and skyscrapers derive satisfaction from knowing that their works will outlive them. Shakespeare, da Vinci, and Picasso are artists whose work, most would argue, will live forever. It is not only the pharaohs, architects, and master builders, however, who participate in symbolic immortality. Bricklayers, iron workers, carpenters, computer programmers, anyone who fashions something out of nothing can derive a sense of satisfaction from the knowledge that their labors will outlive them. Consider the medieval church builders who did not finish their work in their lifetime. Symbolic immortality, a culturally devised solution to the certainty of our own death, is available—and essential—to us all.

Heroism

In a very real way all of us are actors – and heroes. Everyone is playing the leading role in the story of his or her own life, the heroic narrative in which each of us is the protagonist. The classical hero goes into battle, faces death, and survives. Compared with the exploits of, say, Achilles, simply surviving our day-to-day existence might seem an egregious lowering of the heroism bar. Henry

Leonardo DaVinci

David Thoreau wrote, "Most men lead lives of quiet desperation," which doesn't sound especially heroic. But all of us, even in our quietest shapes, are living heroically, or trying to. We must.

Every day we get out of bed and we act. I don't mean that we put on a show or pretend anything. I mean that we take *action*. We do. According to Jean Paul Sartre, we only exist through what we do. He said, "there is no reality except in action. Man is nothing but the sum of his actions…. There is no love apart from the deeds of love; there is no genius other than that which is expressed in works of art." The idea is ancient. Karma is the Sanskrit word for action. You are what you do. You become what you do. You are who you are because of what you've done.

Another great modern philosopher, Louis C.K., has a great riff on *action* as character. In one of his bits he talks about how, when he's flying first class and a soldier comes onto the plane, he imagines himself giving up his seat – but he never does. That doesn't prevent him from luxuriating, briefly, in the warm feeling of what a great guy he is for just having the thought. By poking fun at himself in this way, Louis reminds us that we are what we *do,* and if we don't do anything we're basically just jerks. Descartes had a different view: "I think therefore I am," which makes us wonder if Descartes is the guy who manages to continue to believe what a great guy he is just for thinking that he *might* give up his first-class seat for a soldier. I'm definitely on the side of, "I *act* therefore I am." I vote for *karma*. To act – and I mean this in every sense of the word – is to be heroic. When you thrust yourself into the open and take a stand, when you allow yourself to stick out, when you proclaim to the world that you have something to say and you're going to

Louis C.K.

say it, you make yourself something of a target. You invite people to take shots at you – and they will. That's heroism. That's *individuation*.

The very powerful and necessary urge to individuate is something we all share, but we also have the equally powerful urge to disappear into the crowd, to merge. If individuation lifts us up and makes us stick out from the masses, there is also a kind of gravity that pulls us down and makes us want to merge. We merge with mommy. We merge with our friends and our peers, our families, our lovers. We merge, daily, with our coworkers, our sports teams, our political parties – all those *isms* – that define us and give us *shape.* This is the erotic urge. To individuate and to merge – these are the *twin ontological motives,* which is a fancy way of saying that no matter what you're doing, you're always in the process of doing one or the other.

Culture responds to the unknowable mysteries of existence by answering the three basic questions and passing those answers along to us. Those answers provide the blueprint – the *shape* – of the heroic narrative. The creation and subsequent life-long maintenance of this project of self-invented identity is, in theatrical terms, the central *action* of every human being. The accomplishment of that action provides us with a sense of ourselves as heroic figures, as symbolically immortal. Conversely, failing to accomplish that action threatens a loss of self-esteem and a symbolic death.

We shield ourselves from the truth of existence so that we may *act* – so that we may move forward with agency and without paralysis. All of us, throughout our lives cling, to our heroic narratives, whether modest or grandiose. We drive cars, live in houses, go shopping, and educate our children. It is right and fitting that we do so. The paradox of psychological health is that to function with any equilibrium at all we must engage in a vital lie. We must deny the fact of death in our everyday existence. Ironically, mental health means shutting out the truth. Mental health means narrowing down our capacity for feeling *everything.* Mental health requires us *not* to surrender to the awful truth of our cosmic insignificance.

The artist, however, *must* surrender. To be creative the artist must have the capacity to strip away his or her own psychological armor. The actor, in particular, must be able to take on the shape of whatever character she is portraying, complete with all the death-denying armor that character carries around. The most interesting characters, the most challenging, the ones we most want to play and the ones we most want to watch, are those who come to a moment in the narrative when the vital lie is pierced. In that moment the actor must have the capacity to strip away his or her own armor so as to convey the experience truthfully. The actor who can do no more than suggest the shape of that moment and merely present a simulacrum of that experience is, to use a piece of theatrical jargon, just *indicating* the emotion.

This may help explain why the need for art and artists runs so deep and why art is found in every culture. Art offers opportunities for stripping away culturally constructed veneers in a relatively safe environment. The function of the artist is to stay available, to stand ready to remove the armor, stay exposed, and surrender to the mortal truth of existence. Removing the armor and standing exposed is itself an act of heroism. *Surrender* represents the possibility of unleashing an explosion of creativity and emotion in a splitting of the creative atom when we crack through the shell of our culturally constructed armor, and when the buffering shape of identity gives way to the truth of our existence. Acknowledging these human dynamics and embedding them in our work as artists is the beginning of *raising the stakes*. When we find the courage to individuate, to stand boldly on the stage and ask that we be watched, when we have the heroism to *act*, what we create will have the potential to carry within it a sense of the largeness of life and death.

Building and defending a heroic narrative may not be easy, but in life we have no choice in the matter so it comes "naturally." Recreating our predicament truthfully onstage can be rather difficult. People have been trying to figure out how to do it well for centuries.

PART II

A Brief History of Acting Theories and Techniques

Two

Why We Need a System

In the psychic tug of war between merging and individuating we mostly merge. We go along to get along, safely identifying with this sports team or that political party, wearing the colors, cheering loudly when "we" win.

Actors, by contrast, are desperate heroes called on to perform feats of madness, to stand out – on a stage or in front of a camera – to say, "look at me, I am special, I can do this thing." The audience looks hard, holding back its suspension of disbelief, waiting to be convinced, while the actor struggles to deliver someone else's written word, recreate someone else's choreographed movements, and yet remain truthful to the "character," whatever that is. Stage fright is the appropriate response to such an artificial and psychically dangerous circumstance. It is so much more sensible *not* to walk out there.

Consider everything the actor has to carry around in her head as she steps out onto the stage: She's waiting for her cue, the precise moment when she is to take that step pegged to a specific line or a subtle shift in lights, to music or to a sound effect. Memorized lines must now be spoken in a particular way, conveying meaning and character. Weeks of rehearsal have imbued those lines with subtext; the meaning under the meaning. There is blocking, furniture to navigate around and onto. Then there are other actors with whom the actor interacts. What are those relationships?

All of this is within the world of the play, but underneath it – or perhaps just outside of it – is a relentless stream of information from the real world: "I'm in a theater… there's an audience… who's in the audience? Why didn't my scene partner say that line right? Oh no, he skipped a page… no he didn't… I don't feel good, I think I might be coming down with something… focus…. what's my intention in the scene? Get back in the play… remember to breathe…" and so on.

Somehow we do manage to absorb it all and still perform. The human capacity to hold vast quantities of information in memory and put that knowledge and insight to work on the fly is more than impressive. To put it into perspective, scientists in the field of artificial intelligence have found it enormously difficult to write code that would allow a robot to enter a room and improvise a route around unknown obstacles. After some of those experiments they concluded, "Our systems are pathetic compared to biological systems." Yet the actor lives with the gnawing feeling that she is not quite getting it, that perfection lies somewhere just beyond what she is achieving. We strive to *live in the moment* and to *become the character*. Then, when our own consciousness asserts itself in the scene (as it must, since we are not robots), we feel that we have failed.

James Rhodes describes similar challenges he faces as a concert pianist:

James Rhodes

…playing 120,000 notes from memory in the right order with the right fingers, the right sound, the right pedaling while chat-ting about the composers and pieces and knowing there are critics, recording devices, my mum, the ghosts of the past, all there watching and perhaps most crushingly, the realization that I will never, ever give the

perfect recital. It can only ever, with luck,
hard work and a hefty dose of self-forgive-
ness, be 'good enough'.

How might we go about formulating a technique for doing "it" better? The impulse to organize experience is utterly
human – the world is too big, too chaotic for us to take in
all at once. We look for patterns, for systems that will allow
us to make sense of it all. We look for a way to manage the
terror that comes from overload.

In *Consilience: The Unity of Knowledge*, Edmund O.
Wilson talks about the importance of reduction to the scientific process. "… the breaking apart of nature into its natural
constituents… reductionism is the primary and essential
activity of science. It is the search strategy employed to find
points of entry into otherwise impenetrably complex systems." Should we use a reductionist approach to understand
something as complex as the theater? "Complexity is what
interests scientists in the end, not simplicity. Reductionism
is the way to understand it." The same can be said for artists.
The artist's technique is the pathway toward that complexity.
What then are the techniques that work? How can we successfully manage all the nuts and bolts of such a technique
and somehow deliver a performance that is effective, truthful,
moving, even transcendent?

Starting with the Greeks we see a succession of systems
whose one unifying feature might be an acceptance that the
actor's task is too large, too complex to take in all at once.
Some reduction is needed to focus the mind. If you're standing in the wings mentally bombarded with all the lines, cues,
blocking, meanings, relationships, etc., and with the added
burden of self-doubt that comes from caring what others think
– your parents, the director, your peers – the response might
well be total paralysis. A good strategy might be to identify
a few key elements that can serve as focal points, centers of
attention, guide posts.

In the next chapters I will describe how a succession of
thinkers, teachers, actors, theorists, and directors have at-

Jeff Zinn

tacked this problem of narrowing things down to make the actor's task more manageable. There is a progression from "outside-in" techniques that are almost purely *shape* based, to approaches that allow for the exploration of the character's inner life. This progression of narrowing techniques is mirrored by, or perhaps responsive to, another progression: how character has been portrayed in literature, from the archetypal masks employed by the Greeks, through various iterations of stock types, until we come to the magnificently individuated characters of Shakespeare. Once writers have moved beyond the crude shapes of *Everyman*, *The Clever Slave,* and the *Basely Covetous Man,* we find actors and directors racing to catch up. Shakespeare himself seemed to give voice to frustration with the limitations of his players when he warned them that if they could not deliver a more nuanced performance, "I would as lief the town crier spoke my lines!"

THREE

ARISTOTLE, DIDEROT, DELSARTE, AND FEY

I had studied drama at the University of Virginia with great teachers and we studied Stanislavski technique and Meisner technique and all these different things, and I tried my best, but I was never sure, when I was doing those things, I never understood what you were supposed to be thinking about during the actual performance. Am I supposed to be thinking about the journal that I made for the character? Am I thinking about my "moment before?

Tina Fey

A cting is somehow the easiest and the most difficult of the performing arts. After all, unlike mastering a musical instrument, it is entirely possible that someone with no training might step onto a stage or be placed in front of a camera and deliver a decent or even inspired performance. That's because the actor's essential medium and the clay with which he fashions his art object is himself. Theoretically, then, a person who inhabits a *shape* that is pleasing, or at least interesting to the eye, and whose personality is also appealing or interesting or happens to conform to the shape needed by whoever is responsible for casting, might just deliver a creditable performance. This does happen. But moving beyond the lucky confluence of the casting director's need and the actor's look and persona, the waters start to get choppy. The profusion of acting teachers working out of private studios and the hundreds of undergraduate and graduate theater programs attest to the demand for effective training.

The syllabus for the actor in training is endless and irreducible. Stella Adler's hand-transcribed chart of Stanislavski's system, whose forty numbered items included *attention, beats,* and *emotional memory,* placed *work on one's self* at its base in the number one position. That single entry suggests a daunting program of physical, psychological, and intellectual self-improvement. This may explain candid photographs of movie stars such as James Dean and Marilyn Monroe, dressed in comfortable clothes, curled up with a book, uncharacteristically peering through eyeglasses. They are doing their homework.

"Homework" points toward two distinct ends: During the phase leading up to and including the actual rehearsal period, one cannot take in too much information. We share in–depth table work discussions; delve into the historical context of the play; create a biographical backstory for the character; explore relationships in improvisations; rehearse complicated blocking, choreography, and stage combat sequences until they are embedded in our muscle memory. But that extended, weeks-long (in rare cases months, or even years-long) period is distinct from the moment of taking the stage and from all the moments when one is ON stage. Homework's ultimate end is the performance, but it is not enough to suggest that one should study and study and study and then just launch onto the stage, trusting that the preparation will magically coalesce into a coherent performance. Tina Fey nails the essential question in the above passage, "…what [am I] supposed to be thinking about during the actual performance?"

In the following pages we will be charting a path through both phases; the macro course of study *and* narrowing it all down to a usable technique. I have already tipped my hand in suggesting that the many can be resolved and synthesized into the few: *shape, action, transaction,* and *surrender.* As we work through the various approaches I will be pointing out how and where each of these four elements asserts itself.

Aristotle

When we begin to search for what might be the very earliest theatrical systems we find the Natya Shastra, an Indian compendium that spelled out "rules" for theater, dance, and music. Created around 200 BC, it is based on the much older Gandharva Veda which was probably created around 1700 BC. However even that is prefigured by the Egyptian Remesseum Dramatic Papyrus which describes detailed staging instructions for elaborate religious rituals and was created as early as 2600 BC.

For our purposes, however, we will begin with Aristotle, who I like to think of as the original crazy systematizer. Departing from Plato, who preferred to explain the world in terms of essentials such as Truth and Beauty that exist above and apart from actual worldly existence, Aristotle insisted on looking hard at existence on the physical plane. As he went about carving up the world into categories, he wasn't so much interested in simplifying as he was in cataloging everything under the sun. It was his way of making sense of things, perhaps of learning (and then teaching) answers to the great cosmological questions. His works exhaustively covered the topics of logic, geology, physics, metaphysics, biology, medicine, psychology, ethics, politics, and rhetoric. When he turned his attention to the theater in *Poetics,* he was able to identify 11 important elements: *plot, reversal, recognition, imitation, catharsis, miscalculation, character, theme, diction, melody, and spectacle*, which he narrowed to six: *plot, character, theme, diction, melody, and spectacle.* He went even further to say, "The most important of the six is the arrangement of the incidents of the story." In other words, *plot.*

From Poetics
1. Mythos, or "plot"
2. Ethos, or "character"
3. Dianoia, or "thought," "theme"
4. Lexis, or "diction," "speech"
5. Melos, or "melody"
6. Opsis, or "spectacle"
Also...
• Mimesis, or "imitation," "representation"
• Catharsis, or, variously, "purgation,", "purification," "clarification"
• Peripeteia, or "reversal"
• Anagnorisis, or "recognition," "identification"
• Hamartia, or "miscalculation" also known as "tragic flaw"

Many of Aristotle's elements don't appear to address the specific concerns of the actor. They are much more directed toward the writer, director, designer, or producer. His six essential elements are not like Michael Shurtleff's "12 Guideposts," which are supposed to help the actor navigate a scene or a play. That said, it is useful to cover this ground before moving on to more actor-specific systems. Awareness and understanding of Aristotle's 11 elements surely fall into the macro category of what the actor needs to know.

Aristotle's relationship with, and perhaps understanding of, actors seems to have been somewhat removed, even hostile:

> *Why are theatrical artists generally persons of bad character? Is it because they partake but little of reason and wisdom, because most of their life is spent in the pursuit of the arts which provide their daily needs, and because the greater part of their life is passed in incontinence and often in want, and both these things pre-*

pare the way to villainy?

He seems to have regarded actors as rather unruly and inconvenient necessities (not unlike some contemporary directors I can think of). He complains, for example, about the actor who "…adds stylistic histrionics to overcome shortcomings in the text…." Yet for the actor engaged in "work on one's self" and willing to think outside the box of "the part," there is no part of *Poetics* that is not useful.

Drama itself was defined by Aristotle as *mimesis*, the "imitation of an action." Much of our effort in the theater is directed toward blurring the line between the action and the imitation; we want our imitations to be as real as possible.

Aristotle

We understand plot *(mythos)* to be the deliberate ordering of actions to tell a story. The difference between *plot* and *story* is worth considering. The story takes place in real time with a beginning, middle, and end, but that's not necessarily the way we tell the story. We might begin at the end, then flash back to the beginning and start over. Or we might, as in Harold Pinter's *Betrayal,* tell the story backwards, with each scene occurring in reverse chronology. Or, as in *Death of a Salesman*, we might jump forward and backwards in time, mirroring the mental state of Willy Loman. The events of

Sean Sturnick and
Bates Wilder in
Killer Joe at WHAT

The Iliad take place over the course of only a few weeks towards the end of the Trojan wars and are told in a fairly straightforward progression of events/actions. *The Odyssey*, by contrast, tells the story of Odysseus' return home after the war, but the sequence of events is anything but linear. Rather than plunge directly into the journey of Odysseus, Homer begins with several chapters detailing the predicament of his wife and son left

49

behind. This arrangement of the incidents (plot) allows us to receive a tremendous amount of information and backstory while also building suspense.

Spectacle (*opsis*) captures and holds our attention. It's a car chase; a knock-down, drag-out fight scene in Tracy Lett's *Killer Joe;* it's a drunken Vince smashing bottles against a wall in Sam Shepard's *Buried Child.* Shepard happens to be using that spectacular *action* to reveal Vince's character (ethos), or *shape.* So much more effective than talking about it.

Catharsis translates literally as "purging" or "cleansing." The ideal for Aristotle was for the audience to be *purged* of emotion as if it were something unhealthy to be driven from the body. We can't really know if the actor of Aristotle's day, hidden behind a mask and declaiming at high volume to audiences seated in arenas that held thousands, would have had the desire or the ability to communicate authentic emotion as modern actors strive to do. We can, however, begin to think about *catharsis* as another word for *surrender.*

Speech/diction (*lexis*) and melody/song (*melos*) are elements that would seem to go directly to the actor's physical technique and technical competency – *melos* surely does that. But Aristotle meant something quite different from our common understanding of *diction* (proper vocal technique, pronunciation, articulation, etc.) *Diction* for him was about the quality of the writing, word choice, and use of metaphor.

Thought/theme (*dianoia*) is utterly foundational not only to literature and drama but to all the arts. The notion that every action in the play should support the central idea or theme is common among practitioners from Aristotle straight through to the most modern theorists, including Brecht and Grotowski. This element intersects with another of Aristotle's constructions: *final cause.*

The Four Causes

I will admit to a minor obsession with Aristotle's *four causes.* I have found them to be an immensely satisfying way of thinking about the world and especially theater even though they are not part of the *Poetics* and were not, so far as we know, intended for that application. Rather, they were intended to explain non-human objects. They organize the physical world into:

Material cause: the substance from which a thing is made.
Formal cause: the design of a thing made.
Efficient or Moving cause: the energy with which a thing is made.
Final cause: the purpose for which a thing is made.

Let's use a simple cup to dig more deeply into the four causes. Putting last things first, the *final* cause of the cup – its broad purpose – is to provide a container for holding a substance; probably (but not necessarily) liquid, perhaps (but not necessarily) for drinking. The design of the cup, its *formal* cause, is even more variable. We know that cups come in all shapes and sizes. Ultimately, any given cup design must honor the final cause of a cup. The *material* cause of the cup might be clay, wood, metal, plastic, etc.

We arrive at the concept of a cup. We *need* a cup. We can start to imagine this cup, what it might look like, how it might be shaped. Perhaps we have some materials out of which we can fashion this cup. There's a nice lump of clay sitting on a table. That might become our cup, but we're not there yet. It's not enough to need something that we may come to call a cup, or to imagine its shape, or even to accumulate the materials necessary to begin its fabrication. We need to take *action.* We need to start *doing,* and for that we need to put energy to work creating the cup. A motor or a human must turn a wheel. The motor needs electricity or foot power. The human needs food. We need fire or electricity to heat the clay in a kiln. All of these can be described as embodiments of the *moving* cause. Take away any one of the four causes and the cup cannot exist.

How does this help? Let's say that we want to put on a play. The script can serve as our formal cause. It's the structure on which everything else will hang. That's why we workshop things endlessly before we start investing lots of time, energy, and money (moving causes) in a given project. Material causes are everywhere: lumber, paint, fabric, and makeup. (It often strikes me that theater is equal parts dramaturgy and carpentry.)

Here we come to the point in heading down this Aristotelian rabbit hole. What is the final cause? Why are we doing this? Why did we pick this play? Why did we found this theater? The intersection between the 11 elements of the *Poetics* and the four causes is *dianoia*. We can think of the *dianoia* of a play as its final cause; it is the purpose for which the thing is made. Final cause, *dianoia*, is mission statement.

Notice that in the description of the four causes each one referred to a *thing* that is made. The four causes are generally used to describe things that are fabricated – objects. Not things found in nature and not *people*. Some have found it necessary, when applying the four causes to humans, to introduce the presence of God, but setting aside the theological lens, Aristotle's *final cause* can be extremely useful for exploring character (*ethos*). Thinking about the intersection between Poetics and the four causes offers a way to understand a play's purpose from the perspective of the character and, therefore, the actor. If we grab hold of a character, Willy Loman for example, and ask, "for the purpose of … what?" we are simultaneously asking about Willy's final cause and the shape it takes as a heroic narrative. That *shape* isn't something Willy was granted by God; it's a decision he made about the purpose and function of his own life. Final cause in human beings requires *action*: the construction and defense of the heroic narrative.

Theophrastus

Aristotle designated one of his students, Theophrastus, to succeed him as head of the Lyceum. Like his mentor, Theophrastus pursued scholarship in physics, ethics, and metaphysics and became well known for his work in the field of botany. He also seems to have become fascinated with Aristotle's notion of *character*. His book, *Characters,* delineates thirty different stock characters including *The Insincere Man, The Flatterer, The Garrulous Man, The Boor, The Penny Pincher, The Absent-Minded Man, The Man of Petty Ambition, The Lover of Bad Company,* and so on. All of his characters seem to respond to cosmological question number two: "What are we supposed to do while we're here?"

Theophrastus

Theophrastus is the great granddaddy of shape. Mostly forgotten now, his impact was enormous and lasted for centuries. Even today when we speak of "stock characters" we are referencing what he started. Consider how much this kind of thinking still drives the casting process: "OK, for this project we're going to need a *basely covetous man.*" (Think F. Murray Abraham as Salieri in *Amadeus*.) "We're also going to

F. Murray Abraham as Salieri in *Amadeus*

need a *late learner.*" (Think Mark Rufallo in *You Can Count On Me.*) Of course, casting directors don't use that exact vocabulary, but you get the idea. The actor, then and now, called upon to portray one of these stock characters, is provided with a very clear and strong action: to fulfill the heroic narrative suggested by the character label. Modern versions of stock characters might include hipster, wall street executive, sexy librarian, stoner, construction worker, etc.

Over time, Theoprastus's characters migrate and transmogrify. The numbers shrink and expand. Attellan Farce, around 390 BC, gave us Macchus (who would become Punch), Bucco (the fat man), Manducus (a greedy clown), Samnio (Harlequin), and Pappus (the old man). By 200 BC, Plautus had expanded the four to nine: an old man, a young man, a clever slave, a stupid slave, a hanger-on, a flatterer, a courtesan, a pimp, and a braggart soldier. Plautus's characters would be resurrected for the 1962 Broadway musical, *A Funny Thing Happened on the Way to the Forum.*

There is a temptation to skip over the Middle Ages – the *dark* ages – altogether. Theater is banned by the church, and nothing much seems to happen for at least ten centuries. But the Dionysian festivals that gave birth to the theater in ancient Greece morph into the Saturnalia in the Roman period, emerging as the Feast of Fools, as early as the fifth century Out in the street the theatrical impulse continues

Feast of Fools

to survive and thrive in the form of mimes, troubadours, and *jongleurs.* Theater, it seems, is a hardy weed that will not be snuffed out. Eventually the Mystery and Morality plays revive stock characters (Knowledge, Strength, Fellowship, God, Death, etc.) in plays like *The Summoning of Everyman.* The scholar Jody Enders tells us that beginning in 1303, the French lawyers guild, the *Basochien,* gleefully engaged in theatrics in the service of honing their courtroom skills:

> *When the Basochiens sallied forth to play at litigation, they drew on all the thespian talent that they could muster. Forerunners they were of today's most effective litigators along with their televised descendants, as seen in umpteen courtroom dramas from Perry Mason to the People's Court to Judge Judy…*

Enders reports that in the midst of the church-sanctioned Mystery plays, audiences of the 12th century were likely to find *The Farce of the Fart.* Such entertainments may have been tolerated as a way of drawing (and perhaps keeping) audiences for the main event.

By the 1500s the Italian Commedia dell'arte is in full swing. Theophrastus's thirty-plus characters have been streamlined to less than a dozen: lovers, pompous elders, blustering alpha males, sexy female servants, and trickster male servants. Action is improvised around stock plots. Professional actors in this era are improvisers. The written versions were deemed suitable for amateurs to perform, since their

Commedia Players

job was considered to be relatively easier. Say the lines, wear the mask. We may speculate that there were brilliant actors who imbued their performances with depths of emotion (Harlequin Brando?) but Commedia is, once again, mostly about shape.

The whole *characters* enterprise seems to have eventually gotten a bit out of hand: In 1614 Sir Thomas Overbury published *A Wife: Witty Characters* [83 of them!] *Written by Himselfe and Other Learned Gentlemen His Friends.* The stock characters that morphed and grew over the course of 2000 years were all rather one-dimensional *shapes.* If a character was a "lover" he was unlikely to also be a "late learner." It would take a very special genius to break out of the stock character convention and begin to render human behavior in its infinite variety and complexity.

Shakespeare

In *The Invention of the Human,* Harold Bloom argues that the works of William Shakespeare represent a great divide in the history of *character.* Before Shakespeare we have nothing but archetypes, cardboard cut–outs, representations of idealized forms of human beings, but not the individualized personalities that would be his great gift to literature and indeed to our current way of thinking about ourselves. This is not to say that before Shakespeare human beings were not just as individualized as they are today, but the ability of dramatists to portray those individuals was limited. Bloom is insistent on this point:

> The idea of Western character, of the self as a moral agent, has many sources: Homer and Plato, Aristotle and Sophocles, the Bible and St. Augustine, Dante and Kant, and all you might care to add. Personality, in our sense, is a Shakespearean invention... Are there personalities (in our sense) in the plays of any of Shakespeare's rivals? Marlowe deliberately kept to cartoons... Ben Johnson as deliberately confined himself to ideograms. I have a great taste for John Webster, but his heroines and villains alike vanish when juxtaposed to those of Shakespeare. Scholars attempt to impress on us the dramatic virtues of George Chapman and of Thomas Middleton, but no one suggests that either of them could endow a role with human inwardness.

Shakespeare's actors would need to find ways to portray such complexity and move beyond mere *shape* in the portrayal. Remembering that he was an actor/manager (before the role of *director* had been invented), Shakespeare was clearly frustrated with actors not quite up to speed when he wrote:

William Shakespeare

> Speak the speech I pray you as I pronounced it to you, trippingly on the tongue; but if you mouth it as many of your players do, I had as lief the town-crier spoke my lines. Nor do not saw the air too

much with your hand thus, but use all gently; for in the very torrent, tempest, and, as I may say, whirlwind of your passion, you must acquire and beget a temperance that may give it smoothness.

Of course we have no recorded performances from this era. We do, however, have the films of Laur-

Richard Burbage

ence Olivier, John Gielgud, and John Barrymore. These actors were the direct inheritors of an acting tradition that began with Shakespeare, and those performances offer clues as to how subsequent generations of actors passed along the established conventions of the craft. Olivier made this very point in his book, *On Acting*. He wrote about how very short the distance is from Richard Burbage (1567-1619), the originator of Hamlet, Lear, and most of the other great Shakespearean roles, to himself, linking in generational hops through David Garrick (1717-1779), Edmund Kean (1787-1833), and Henry Irving (1838-1905). In Olivier's telling of that journey from Shakespeare's time to the current day, a common theme emerges: the tension between surface and depth, bombast and realism, exterior and interior. In each generation the "great" actor is lauded for his ability to move the audience with an ever greater sense of truth. A contemporary critic, Richard Flecknoe, observed that:

Burbage was a delightful Proteus [in The Two Gentlemen of Verona*], so wholly transforming himself into his part, putting off himself with his clothes, as he never... assum'd himself again until the play was done....*

Olivier writes of the more than 100-year gap between Burbage and Garrick as a time "when the theater had been lulled to sleep by sweet tones: beautiful voices, lyricism; romantic, hollow, sweet cadences signifying little." Then Garrick bursts onto the scene with "…dare we say a hint of reality?" He appears to have been the first to insist on a rehearsal period of more than five days. Of Edmund Kean, Olivier says, "I think his approach was probably the nearest we have to the modern theater of today. A Reality… I think he opened their eyes to the truth and thrilled them out of the boxes." He notes Henry Irving's dedication and commitment to making a life in the theater before going on to speak of how he, Olivier, was inspired by the Hamlet of American actor John Barrymore (1882-1942), nearly Olivier's contemporary. "It seemed to me that he breathed life into the character, which, since Irving, had descended into arias and false inflections – all very beautiful and poetic, but castrated. Barrymore put back the balls." Olivier clearly viewed Barrymore as a modern, bringing new life and "balls" to a field grown stale. Yet when we watch the clip of Barrymore recreating his "To be or not to be" from the 1941 bit of Hollywood fluff, *Playmates,* (look for it on YouTube) we wince at the over-the-top style, the too-busy eyebrows, the melodramatic pausing for effect. This is not what most 21st century audiences would consider, "A Reality." The yearning for ever more truthful techniques continues. Not to denigrate them or to imply that they do not move us, Olivier's own great performances are, above all, triumphs in the art of *shape*. They certainly entertain us. His Archie Rice, by all accounts, was a tour de force; his Nazi dentist in *Marathon Man* is delightfully sinister.

John Barrymore

From Theophrastus until the early 20th century, acting technique is dominated by *shape*. Despite the fact that Shakespeare created a universe populated with intensely individuated characters, it would take another 400 years for the acting profession to catch up with his great genius and develop a way of bringing those characters to authentic, truthful life.

The epochal handoff may be said to have taken place on the set of *Marathon Man,* where Olivier, the great inheritor of the old-school, outside-in tradition, crossed paths and traded jabs with Dustin Hoffman, by then an exemplar of the Method. As the story goes, Hoffman showed up on the set, bleary-eyed after a night of carousing at Studio 54. Apparently he offered this information to Olivier as something of an explanation/excuse for his condition, which happened to match the damaged state of Hoffman's character, and not as some kind of deliberate technique/preparation for the role. The story goes that Olivier quipped something along the lines of, "Have you ever tried acting, dear boy?" Even if apocryphal, the story is delicious precisely because of the implicit conflict between the two traditions, one departing and the other arriving.

After Shakespeare's death in 1616 our historical focus shifts back across the channel to France with the birth in 1622 and subsequent career of Jean-Baptiste Poquelin, aka Molière. That Shakespeare's works would be eclipsed for a time was almost inevitable given the advent of the Puritan movement in England and the closing of all London theaters in 1642. The Globe Theater was demolished in 1644.

As prodigious and brilliant as Molière's body of work may have been – he wrote and produced 36 plays in 28 years including *The Miser, Tartuffe, The Misanthrope,* and *The Imaginary Invalid* – in some ways his ascension can be seen as something of a setback, to the acting profession at least, if not to dramatic literature. After all, Moliere was essentially building on the conventions of Commedia dell'arte with its collection of stock

Molière

characters, all of whom demanded to be rendered in broad strokes. This shape-driven approach was further cemented when, shortly after Moliere's death in 1673, La Comedie-Française was founded by decree of Louis XIV, essentially becoming the state theater of France.

We might thank the French revolution for disrupting the status quo and paving the way for another revolution in the way actors would portray their characters. Jean–Jacques Rousseau prompted an explosion of thinking and writing when he published his *Discourse on Inequality* in 1755. This book is not the venue to fully explore the currents and cross–currents that erupted in Europe and America, whose own revolution was an inspiration to the French. I only suggest that a theater heavily influenced and dominated by aristocratic tastes and customs of the court was about to give way to a theater that might better portray ordinary human beings.

Diderot

The first really thorough dissertation on acting is probably Denis Diderot's, *The Paradox of Acting*, written in the late 1700s but not translated into English until 1883. Standing on the shoulders of Descartes, whose preoccupation with the mind/body split formed the basis of "dualism," Diderot frames the problem for the actor as a battle between intelligence and passion. Jane Austen used the labels *Sense and Sensibility* to describe those fundamental governing entities. It was already a given that the actor must possess ample quantities of both. Diderot's position was that sensibility – or shall we say, *surrender* – must be ruled by sense. As the English actor Henry Irving summed it up in the introduction to the translation, "The extravagant creature who loses her self control has no hold on us; that is gained by the man who is self controlled.... You may have your sublime moments, but they must come when the man of genius is hovering between nature and his sketch of it and keeping a watchful eye on both."

The insistence on a controlling intelligence might suggest that performances were still rather mechanical and presentational, and they probably were. A palpable hunger for more naturalistic approaches can be found in the writing of other theater practitioners.

By around 1800, François-Joseph Talma, a leading actor of the Comédie-Française, had already broken new ground by demanding appropriate period costuming and scenic elements. Until then a character in a Roman tragedy would have been clothed in contemporary fancy court dress. That puts togas on the cutting edge of costume design in 1750. Talma also banned

Denis Diderot

the practice of allowing privileged audience members to place their chairs directly on the stage. Garrick had insisted on the same prohibition at the Theatre Royal, Drury Lane in London, almost fifty years earlier.

In 1825 Talma contributed his own treatise called *On The Actor's Art*. His essay was an early effort to satisfy the need for "...a permanent embodiment of the principles of our art; a kind of vade mecum [manual] of the actor's calling, written by one of themselves." He devoted much of the essay to an appraisal of Le Kain (Henri Louis Cain, 1728-1778), who had abandoned the conventional declamatory style and moved toward a more natural delivery of the text. The core message to the actor from both Talma and Diderot was that passion should be controlled by intelligence; sense and sensibility in balance, with sense winning the day. It's probably not a coincidence that Jane Austen's novel of that title was published in 1811. The tension between these two elements had become part of the cultural conversation.

Shape, whatever it is guided by, was still very much in vogue and would stay that way for some time. We think of British acting styles, particularly in the 18th and 19th centuries, as shape-driven and presentational, but the French were even more extreme. As late as 1897 George Bernard Shaw, wearing his ruthless-critic hat, lashed out at the Paris Conservatory, where actors were "…taught that there is one 'right' way (all others 'wrong')" of executing the routine tasks of walking and talking, sitting and standing, entering and exiting. Ironically enough, the Conservatory had been founded as an expression of the revolution in 1795. The curriculum, however, was still bound up in the stale conventions of an era defined by Molière.

All the emphasis on "intelligence" was probably an overreaction to the fear that actors might get carried away with their own emotions or, put another way, that *surrender* would take over. Diderot's breakthrough in proposing the incorporation of "intelligence" into technique was to suggest a process in which the actor considers all the elements of a performance. The actor in the wings, then and now, "hovering between nature and his sketch of it," stands ready to ride the rollercoaster of the script hoping to navigate the waters intelligently but somehow finding the passion to inspire a living performance. This has never been an easy thing to do, and theater people have looked for help wherever they could find it.

Theater, Science, Politics

The theater is always sensitive to the currents of its time and seems to draw on contemporary scientific theory to explain itself. The psychological theory prevalent from Aristotle's time up to and including the 19th century was that human behavior and motivation were controlled by fluids in the body known as *humours*: black bile, yellow bile, phlegm, and blood. The transition from the 18th to the 19th century brought explosions of change in science and technology, politics, religion, philosophy, and psychology. The virtues of efficiency and systemization introduced along with the First Industrial Revolution were finding their way into all corners of western culture.

Around 1800 a theory of brain structure, first called *Organology* and later *Phrenology*, was developed by the German physician Franz Joseph Gall and became a cultural phenomenon. Gall argued that the brain is divided into a large number of functional organs, each responsible for particular human mental abilities and dispositions: hope, love, spirituality, greed, language, the ability to detect the size, form, and color of objects, etc. Almost 100 years later Stanislavski would incorporate into his system the "affective memory" experiments of French psychologist Theodule Armand Ribot. Rebranding it *emotional memory*, Stanislavski hoped to offer a scientific basis for unlocking the secrets of *surrender.*

We may also conjecture that the transition from a formal presentational style to a more naturalistic approach in the theater was influenced by the dynamics at play in the French Revolution. The 10 bloody years from 1789 to 1799 saw the formality of the Court overrun by the authenticity of the commoner. It is somewhat ironic that the passage from declamation to naturalism made the actor's task more, not less, difficult. When rules are rigid, they are easier to follow. A naturalistic style leaves the actor to his own devices, adrift in a sea of his own instincts, memories, and passions.

Delsarte

François Delsarte came along in 1811 with a highly systematized catalogue of facial expressions, body postures, and gestures designed to dictate in the most granular terms the best way to express each of the innumerable varieties of human desire, motivation, and emotion. This was to be the apotheosis of sense and sensibility, merged in ideal shapes. Delsarte's charts depicting expressions of the eyebrows, noses, hands, legs, etc. are easily ridiculed today, but at the time they caused a sensation and were widely embraced. The Delsarte style of acting found its way into the early silent films of D.W. Griffith and others. Since these were essentially pantomimes, a gestural shorthand worked well to make up for the lack of dialogue.

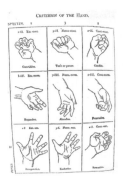

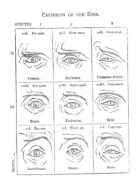

Delsarte's system became an international phenomenon with various acolytes pedaling their own versions and derivations. The system was purported to be more than an acting technique; it was a blueprint for living. Another chart shows a complex matrix of concentric circles and interlocking wheels with legends such as *contemplation sympathy, conscience – sentiment, judgment, sensation – intuition, instinct, induction.* Three pillars labeled *will, memory, intelligence* appear to support the other elements. A veneer of religiosity suffuses the whole, with the inscrutable *circumincession of the faculties type* suggesting that this was somehow connected to the holy trinity. Delsarte's system eventually fell out of fashion and was increasingly ignored. Today there are some who complain that he was misunderstood and that his system still has both relevance and utility for the modern practitioner.

Delsarte's system lives on primarily as a relic of an extreme, *shape*-driven approach. But Delsarte's life story yields insight into the driven heroic narrative of an artist rather desperately attempting to make sense of a world that threatened to come apart around him at crucial moments in his biography. As told in *The Delsarte Recitation Book,* he and his brother were orphaned when both parents died in poverty:

François Delsarte

The winter of 1821 was unusually severe in Paris. One night, in a deserted loft, two little boys entwined in each other's arms lay fast asleep. The sleep of one of them was eternal and when morning broke, Francois Delsarte was hugging to his heart the starved and frozen body of his brother...

Overcome with grief and perhaps delirious from hunger, he has a kind of seizure and then

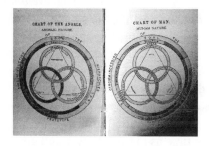

Reviving from the fit, his senses were suddenly entranced by a vision. Exquisite forms and colors floated before his eyes; a wondrous ecstasy filled his mind; celestial music cried into his ears and flooded his soul with harmonies, which he afterward said haunted him through life....

When he was twelve years old an older man, a musician, noticed him "making strange signs in the sand" while a marching band played nearby. Asked what the signs might signify Delsarte answered, "...I have here written the music of the soldiers." The musical savant was rescued from the gutter, accepted into the Paris Conservatory, eventually married the daughter of the director of the "Grand Opera House," and became rich and famous. Quite the heroic narrative. But then came the experience that disrupted the narrative and challenged the original *causa sui* project:

> *After a few years of marvelous success, and when his artistic prospects were extraordinary, he lost his voice entirely for one year. He was obliged to abandon his career upon the stage, and forced to earn his living as a private teacher instead of as a public performer. It was this calamity, or what appeared as such at that time, which led Delsarte to his grand and noble career; for it induced him to search after a natural and scientific basis for art, which eventually made him the greatest master of expression.*

Delsarte's heroic narrative is classically protean as he moves from "impoverished urchin" to "gifted prodigy" to "accomplished success." The narrative has a clear trajectory until it is broken – suddenly, unexpectedly – by the loss of his voice, his gift. His *causa sui* is destroyed and must be reinvented, this time as master teacher and guru.

Art never exists in a vacuum, and it is not a coincidence that Delsarte's system came along during the time of the Second Industrial Revolution, when anything and everything was being systematized, rationalized, and mechanized. But the pendulum was bound to swing the other way.

FOUR

THE MOVE TOWARD TRUTH

In the 1700s star performers such as Talma led the way by insisting on a more historically accurate, naturalistic approach to setting and costume. In the 19th century it took Georg II, Duke of Saxe-Meiningen, and André Antoine's Théâtre Libre to develop a directors' theater in which all elements of the mise en scène would be rendered with historical accuracy. Saxe-Meiningen staged elaborate crowd scenes that startled audiences because each person on stage was individuated. But it was the plays of Ibsen and Strindberg, with their recognizable contemporary characters with everyday concerns, that opened the door for Antoine and others to begin bringing the stories of authentic human beings to the stage.

André Antoine

Stanislavski

Théâtre Libre and the Meiningen Ensemble were at the theatrical cutting edge when young Konstantin Sergeyevich

Alexeiev, the son of a wealthy Moscow merchant, started acting in the fully equipped playhouse built by his father for the amusement of his friends and family. Since the acting profession was held in even lower esteem in Russia than in the rest of Europe, Konstantin adopted the stage name Stanislavski to keep his burgeoning career a secret. Stanislavski studied for a short time at the Moscow Theatre School, very much in the mold of the Comédie-Française, with its stock poses and artificial gestures. Elsewhere in the cultural landscape a new movement, naturalism, was taking hold in the writing of Pushkin and Gogol and in the performances of Shchepkin at the Maly Theater.

With Shchepkin, the corner on Diderot was turned. No longer was the actor standing at a remove from the character, offering a carefully controlled representation of sensibility guided by sense. Shchepkin stated, "It is so much easier to play mechanically – for that you only need your reason. But an actor of feeling – that's quite different…In the first case you need only pretend to live – in the second you really have to live." Stanislavski was surely influenced by Shchepkin, who had dominated the Moscow theater scene for decades. In 1882 Stanislavski experienced a further awakening while watching a performance of *Othello* by the Italian actor Tommaso Salvini:

Stanislavski

> *How simple, clear, beautiful, and tremendous was everything that Salvini did and showed! But why was it that when I saw Salvini I remembered Rossi and the great Russian actors whom I had seen? Why did I feel that all of them had something in common, something I seemed to know very well… What was it?*

Like Delsarte, Stanislavski became consumed with codifying the creative process. In *Science and the Russian Tradition*, Jonathan Pitches relates this urge to the Newtonian method gaining popularity at the time, of searching for "underlying causes of events in the empirical world." Stanislavski took this approach to heart and incorporated it into his life's work. Ribot's experiments in *affective memory* – the triggering of emotions through the reactivation of long-dormant memories – seemed to offer a technical solution to the actor's daunting task of summoning emotion at will. Here was another example of using science to access the art.

The System

To read Stanislavski is to encounter a comprehensive technique that is almost overwhelming in its breadth and complexity. The chart of Stanislavski's system, as transcribed by Stella Adler in 1934, would fill a wall. After dividing the work of the actor into the super categories *Inner* and *Outer*, he went further, enumerating dozens of subcategories. The essence of Stanislavski's chart – and his system – returns us to Diderot's paradox. At the top of the chart we see (E) *THE PART* with (C) *COMPLETE INTERNAL INNER FEELING* and (D) *COMPLETE EXTERNAL* connected by (A) *TRANSACTION*. In other words, the separate and competing worlds of inner sensibility and outer sense must somehow be negotiated and pulled together into the whole of *The Part*. Off to the side we see (B) *SPINE,* which is Stanislavski's jargon for the overall purpose and meaning of the play. Might *Spine* also be labeled *dianoia* or *final cause*? I believe it could.

Robert (Bobby) Lewis believed the chart important enough to include as a foldout in his book, *Method or Madness*. He described it as "simply an attempt to put down in some organized form what good actors are doing when they're acting well." That's all well and good, but Stanislavski's system is too complex, has too many moving parts to function as a technique that might carry the actor confidently onto the stage and through the play. It is better read as a suggested curriculum for an actor's

Jeff Zinn

total training. It would fall to Stanislavski's descendants – Lee Strasberg, Stella Adler, Sanford Meisner, Uta Hagen and others – to transform the *system* into a *method*. Each of them would draw from the system the elements they felt were most central and essential, in many cases leaving the rest behind. Before we explore their solutions, insights, and specific techniques, I want to stay with Stanislavski a bit longer.

As Lewis observed, the chart is laid out like a pipe organ, with a "great foot pedal" across the bottom labeled *work on*

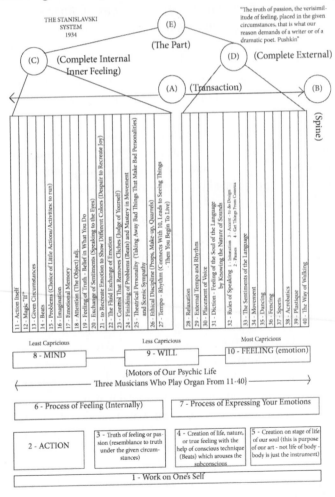

one's self. Not "oneself," mind you, but "one's self." This suggests that Stanislavski recognized the need for the actor to think about, identify, and "work on" the *self* before engaging the character –

1- Work on One's Self

---

the part – as a separate entity.

Moving up the chart, the next tier reads:

> 2 – *Action*
> 3 – *Truth of feeling or passion (resemblance to truth under the given circumstances)*
> 4 – *Creation of life, nature, or true feeling, with the help of conscious technique (beats) which arouses the subconscious*
> 5 – *Creation on stage of life of our Soul (this is purpose of our art – not life of body – body is just the instrument)*

2 - ACTION	3 - Truth of feeling or passion (resemblance to truth under the given circumstances)	4 - Creation of life, nature, or true feeling with the help of conscious technique (Beats) which arouses the subconscious	5 - Creation on stage of life of our soul (this is purpose of our art - not life of body - body is just the instrument)

Notice the primacy of *action,* which is given no further explanation. Numbers 3, 4, and 5 all contain words like *truth, passion, feeling, true feeling, soul,* and *art. Truth* establishes the now common phrase, *under the given circumstances.* Number 4 introduces the concept of *beats* as the building blocks of a conscious technique. Aristotle established *plot* as a sequence of actions. Stanislavski mirrors this with his own sequence of *beats,* which we may think of as small actions.[*]

---

[*] There is some amusing lore connected to the word *beats.* In his conversations with Stella Adler and other Americans, Stanislavski actually said *bits* and was misheard and misunderstood because of his Russian accent, which transformed *bits* into *beets.* We know this because in the Russian edition of *An Actor Prepares,* Stanislavksi used the word *kouski,* which translates as "bits or pieces." In English the word *beat* has a musical connotation. We tend, therefore, to use the term to mean both *unit,* as in "let's do the next beat," and also musically, as in "OK, take a beat."

The next tier gets specific as it resolves into two distinct elements: 6 – *Process of feeling (internally)* and 7– *Process of expressing your emotion.*

6 - Process of Feeling (Internally)	7 - Process of Expressing Your Emotions

Now we're back to Diderot and Cartesian dualism. Sense and sensibility. Stanislavski goes beyond Diderot when he states that not only is the actor governed by the forces of sense and sensibility in tension, the actor's sensibility must be ruled by his intelligence. Stanislavski develops a working approach to that task, breaking down which aspect of the actor's craft is connected to each side of the equation. These two sides are mirrored and reinforced at the top of the chart, reaching down to bracket the two banks of "pipes" with the labels C (*Complete Internal – Inner Feeling*) and D (*Complete External.*)

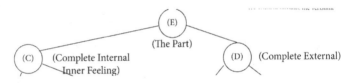

The tier with 8 – *Mind*, 9 – *Will*, and 10 – *Feeling* in the center of the chart further compartmentalizes the parts of our consciousness that allow us to take action. The labels *least capricious (Mind), less capricious (Will),* and *most capricious (Feeling)* seem slightly out of whack, perhaps as a result of Adler's imperfect stenography. I would have said that the will was less capricious than the mind, but let's move on.

Exploring the two banks of pipes on our pipe organ, again, the left bank is labeled 6 – *Process of Feeling (Internally)* and the right bank is labeled *7 – Process of Expressing Your Emotion.*

6 - Process of Feeling (Internally)	7 - Process of Expressing Your Emotions

The thirteen elements that make up the right side all focus on the mechanics of *shape: Relaxation; External Tempo & Rhythm; Placement of Voice; Diction – Feeling of the Soul of the Language by Knowing the Nature of Sounds; Rules of Speaking; The Sentiments of the Language,* and end with a sequence of physical disciplines, *Movement; Dancing; Fencing; Sports; Acrobatics.*

We are now squarely in the conservatory and well away from what usually comes to mind when we think of Stanislavski whose name typically conjures up the "internal" side of the pipe organ, not these overtly physical disciplines. We can see how central *action* is to Stanislavski's system, because it appears twice on the chart (the only element to have that distinction.) It appears as number 2 in the second tier just above *Work on One's Self* and then as number 11, the first in the left bank of pipes labeled *Complete Internal.*

Somewhat surprising is that nowhere on the chart do we find the words *objective, intention,* or even *motivation,* since, in common practice, those words are often substituted for the word *action.* Bobby Lewis was especially fond of *intention* and defined it as "what really is happening on the stage regardless of what you are saying." (Later, in the chapter on *Action,* I will talk about the difference between *objective, intention,* and *motivation.*)

Stanislavski intended his system to be holistic. All four of the elements that I consider key – *shape, action, transaction,* and *surrender* – are embedded in the chart, but there's no denying that the system's emphasis is on *surrender*: unleashing the inner, emotional life. Numbers 6 and 7 on the third tier are the giveaways: The left bank of 17 pipes is labeled *Process of Feeling (Internally),* whereas the right bank of 13 is labeled *Process of Expressing Your Emotions.* In other words, the whole thing is ultimately about either conjuring or expressing emotion. This belies the assertion that the Stanislavski system is truly "holistic" and reinforces the notion that it's all about finding the pathways to *surrender.*

The Other Russians

Stanislavski's impact on acting is indisputable. What I like to call the "Stanislavski family tree" continues to flower with generations of students still studying the system in the many forms it has spawned. In his own day Stanislavski's impact was enormous,

not just as the architect of an acting system but as a producer and director. In 1897 he and Vladimir Nemirovich Danchenko founded the Moscow Art Theater (M.A.T.), which survives and thrives to this day. The M.A.T.'s reputation was made when, starting in 1898, Stanislavski directed Anton Chekhov's *The Seagull, Uncle Vanya, Three Sisters,* and *The Cherry Orchard.* These plays were written and produced in reaction – and perhaps as an antidote – to the popular melodramas then common in the Russian theater. The new movement was Naturalism, and Stanislavski embraced it with a vengeance. Inspired by André Antoine's Théâtre Libre and Meiningen's ravishing spectacles, Stanislavski took everything he knew about the theater, everything he had seen and stud-

Anton Chekhov

ied, and poured it into the work of the M.A.T. In *The Stanislavski Technique: Russia, a Workbook for Actors*, Mel Gordon
describes Stanislavski's "super-realistic lighting and sound ef-
fects." But a symphony of crickets chirping was apparently not
to Chekhov's liking. The playwright would later say that "the
'mosquito swatting' atmosphere... very nearly ruined [my]
play."

Chekhov had been introduced to Stanislavski by Vladimir Nemirovich-Danchenko, whose own play, *The Worth of
Life*, had been chosen over *The Seagull* (which had flopped
at the Maly) for a prestigious theater award. To his credit,
Nemirovich-Danchenko recognized Chekhov's play as the
superior work. *The Seagull* was
chosen as the inaugural M.A.T.
production and proved to be a
sensation. Chekhov was subsequently commissioned to write
*Uncle Vanya, The Cherry Or-
chard,* and *The Three Sisters*.
To this day the M.A.T. logo is
a seagull. It is not an exaggera-
tion to say that the support of
Stanislavski and Nemirovich-
Danchenko propelled Chekhov
from the physician, short-story

Vsevolod Meyerhold

writer, theater dabbler he had been, to the essential figure of
dramatic literature he is today.

Just as Stanislavski worked to overturn the theatrical
conventions of an earlier time, some of the artists trained by
Stanislavski and working within the M.A.T. began to strain
against naturalism and what was starting to feel like the locked-
in style of the M.A.T. It is fitting that Vsevolod Meyerhold
played Treplev, the character who rails against convention
and calls for "new forms" in *The Seagull*. Meyerhold would
go on to form his own studio, experimenting with radical staging techniques and acting approaches that broke starkly with
Stanislavski's approach. His technique of "Biomechanics" was
also intensely *shape* driven.

Heavily influenced by Frederick Taylor, author of *The Principles of Scientific Management*, and aligning his theory with the needs of the new Soviet Union, Meyerhold declared:

> *The actor embodies in himself both the organizer and that which is organized (i.e. the artist and his material). The formula for acting may be expressed as follows: N = A1 + A2 (where N = the actor; A1 = the artist who conceives the idea and issues the instructions necessary for its execution; A2 = the executant who executes the conception of A1). The actor must train his material (the body), so that it is capable of executing instantaneously those tasks that are dictated externally (by the actor, the director...). Since the art of the actor is the art of plastic forms in space, he must study the mechanics of his body.*

Another former student and M.A.T. company member whose influence is still felt today was Michael Chekhov, whom Stanislavski designated to lead the second M.A.T. company. Chekhov, like Meyerhold, strained against the limitations of an overly naturalistic approach and devised a technique he named *Psychological Gesture.* My earliest training in the theater was with Ronald Bennett, an actor who had studied and performed with the Michael Chekhov Company in England and America. Our classes were intense physical workouts using *psychological gesture* exercises:

Michael Chekhov

From my notes at the time:

We warm up with a series of movements, movements are first executed staccato, very fast and precise, and then legato, basically in slow motion. The aim is to involve the whole body in a focused way. The class then moves to the outer perimeter of the room. Bennett calls out a word: *fear, joy, panic, confidence.* With that as prompt, the students move quickly toward the center of the room and form a human sculpture.

There was to be no thinking, no designing

the shapes in the mind beforehand, no imposition of a formal cause. The word called out was itself *dianoia or theme.* Formal cause/design/shape arose spontaneously in the act of moving into position.

Much of the training was classic right-side-of-the-chart stuff: vocal training, dance, fencing. Bennett's direction was always no nonsense: "Create strong forms!" "Energy!" It was fun to do, but I had to unlearn most of it when I

Ronald Bennett

got to New York, where the going style was much more in the Stanislavski mode. At my very first audition I did a few lines of Shakespeare in the high-voltage style I had learned from Bennett. "Sweetie," the director Crystal Field, gently prompted, "here we go for naturalism." I made the adjustment (and got the part.) In his attempts to break new ground

Michael Chekhov was following the lead of Stanislavski, who was always moving forward, always reinventing his system. In exploring other ways of expressing truthful emotion we can discern in Chekhov what is almost a nostalgia for the older classical forms: Commedia, melodrama, even Delsarte. Using *psychological gesture* to short circuit the brain's executive function, Chekhov prefigures Meisner and even Grotowski.

The American descendants of Stanislavski seem to have understood that the system needed pruning and so focused on the elements they felt were most central and most useful. Number 16 – *Imagination* would be seized on by Stella Adler. She insisted that Stanislavski himself had revealed this "truth" to her in the series of private sessions she had with him in Paris that produced the chart. Even today the "Stella Adler Studio of Acting" website proclaims:

Stella Adler

> *Actors' imaginations are the most powerful source for them to draw on. To bring alive a mimetic narrative – a story that happens as it is told – an actor must be able to create not just a replication of the actual, but a transforming, living experience. To create such an experience, Adler Studio actors are asked to use their imagination to locate the fullest range of motivational force, rather than depending solely on observation and emotional memory.*

The two teachers in the direct line from Stanislavski who have probably had the most influence on contemporary acting technique are Lee Strasberg and Sanford Meisner. Their students and the students of their students have influenced acting styles and approaches to the teaching of acting world-wide and still dominate the firmament of actors and directors in the United States.

The Fervent Years

When Harold Clurman, Sanford Meisner, and Lee Strasberg found themselves playing bit parts for the Theater Guild in 1925, the Broadway theater was calcified. The Guild had aspired to be the go-to venue for interesting new work, but as Clurman wrote, "All the productions were rather pretty (with a kind of disguised middle-class stuffiness) and they nearly always lacked passion or pointedness." Strasberg and Meisner saw an opening and were passionate about the possibilities. Both had taken classes at the American Laboratory Theater with Richard Boleslavsky (whom Clurman called "a truant from the Moscow Art Theater") and Maria Ouspenskia, and they were beginning to soak up the new Stan-

Harold Clurman

islavski system. Clurman described the young Lee Strasberg: "He talked mostly about acting, upon which he seemed as concentrated as a jeweler over the inner mechanism of a watch. I never dreamed that there was that much to it." Clurman's own vision was somewhat broader:

> ...my study and observation of theatre practice grew more systematic. While I studied, I talked. Indeed, I preached. What I insisted on at first was an elaboration of Strasberg's point of view - a point of view not original with him, of course, but one which he had made convincing to me. Its pivotal thesis was that the so-called interpretative elements of the theatre were really creative functions, so that plays were to be seen as artistic wholes, not as scripts adorned by acting and direction.

79

In other words, Clurman homed in on the dianoia/final cause of a play. All of the other "interpretive elements" would be in service to that cause.

The Group Theater was born in "the fervent years," as the roaring '20s were sputtering out, and came into its own as the Great Depression took hold. The Group's founders wanted the new theater to engage the important issues of the day. That would require an acting style that was realistic and, above all, truthful. The stilted artifice that still lingered as a relic of the established theater of Europe was old news. Americans were ready for Strasberg, Meisner, and Elia Kazan. In a few years they would get to know Eli Wallach, Rod Steiger, Shelley Winters, Marlon Brando, Marilyn Monroe, and other descendants and disciples of the Stanislavski family tree. The Group was born in 1931, but the passion that had driven its formation would prove difficult to sustain. By 1936 it was all but dead. In a preview of things to come, the Group Theater Studio came into existence in 1937. Hundreds auditioned for only 50 spots in the exclusive workshop led by Strasberg, Kazan, and Meisner. Ten years later, The Actors Studio was officially formed. It was headed by Strasberg, Bobby Lewis, and Cheryl Crawford, who had also been the administrative brains behind the Group Theater.

Lee Strasberg and The Actors Studio

The Actors Studio has been housed in a former church on West 44th Street since 1955. From about 1979 to 1981 I was privileged to observe the twice-weekly sessions that have met there religiously (pun intended) since its founding. At each session the permanent members, inducted by audition, present scenes to the assembled audience of members and observers. At the conclusion of the scene the moderator gives notes and invites comment from the members. The active moderators during the time I was there included Ellen Burstyn, Arthur Penn, Elia Kazan, Shelley Winters, Harold Clurman, and Lee Strasberg. Observers were sometimes recruited to participate in scene work. At one Friday session, with Strasberg moderating, I found myself playing the role of Nick in *Who's Afraid of Virginia Woolf*. I don't remember much about that session or whether Lee addressed any of his comments to me. I do recall that it was terrifying.

Lee Strasburg

I studied acting with several teachers who were Studio members including David Garfield, who wrote *The Actors Studio: A Player's Place*, and Susan Batson, whose own book about acting, *Truth: Personas, Needs, and Flaws...*, was published in 2007. I had been observing at the Studio for several months when a friend invited me to a class she was taking with Batson. Like most actors in New York, I had taken my share of acting classes, bouncing around from teacher to teacher. Studying with Susan was different from any of those experiences. At least three times each week we would arrive at her tiny apartment on the Upper West Side, usually around 9 or 10 in the morning. Each class would last at least four hours and often all day. We would sit on the floor while, one by one, students would get up and work on a monologue, song, or poem. As the rest of us watched, the student would interact with Susan.

Susan Batson

Essentially the process was about stripping away, opening up, breaking down the actor until the tears were flowing, the voice was roaring. Susan would demand that the actor dig down to the deepest layers of hurt and pain: "DO THE WORK! ... CUT THE BULLSHIT! ... WHAT IS THE NEED?" she would scream, and we would dig deeper and deliver more.

I had always had trouble going to *that place* inside myself. I had read books by and about Stanislavski. I had done sense memory exercises where I tasted tastes and smelled smells from experiences in my childhood. But it wasn't until Susan pushed me down, deep inside myself that I found myself dripping in tears and snot, or roaring like a lion – at least in her living room. The takeaway for me, both from my time at Susan's and at the Studio, was that it was all about the *tears*. It was ALL about *surrender*. Everything else was secondary. At the Studio there seemed to be an appreciation that all of the many pipes on the Stanislavski organ – voice, diction, movement – were important, but no one was ever really *doing the work* until the tears came and the most primal emotions could be made visible on stage.

In *The Fervent Years*, Clurman makes this very point. For Strasberg, authentic *emotion* was all:

> *The first effect ...on the actors was that of a miracle... Here at last was a key to that elusive ingredient of the stage, true emotion. And Strasberg was a fanatic on the subject of true emotion. Everything was secondary to it. He sought it with the patience of an inquisitor, he was outraged by trick substitutes, and when he had succeeded in stimulating it, he husbanded it, fed it, and protected it. Here was something new to most of the actors, something basic, something almost holy. It was a revelation in the theatre; and Strasberg was its prophet.*

Why not make that the focus? When actors tap into the depths of their own emotions the audience, too, is moved. It is also true that many of the great studio actors had skill that went far beyond expressing emotion. Some of

Julie Harris in *The Beauty Queen of Leenane* at WHAT

our greatest shape-shifting character actors, such as Eli Wallach and Robert Duvall, are or were members. Julie Harris was a member, although when you watch her in *East of Eden* with James Dean, it seems they are from two distinct eras of the theater. At that time, though still relatively young, she was already a Broadway grand dame, and Dean was a classic method mumbler. They were almost in different movies. The Studio was perhaps a magnet for talent more than it was a school for talent. In the end it was, and still is, a place where actors could focus intently on their craft, even if they were stumbling in the dark.

Sanford Meisner

At the Actors Studio it was all about *surrender*. Across town at the Neighborhood Playhouse, Sandy Meisner concentrated on another of Stanislavski's elements, number 20 on the chart: *The Exchange Of Sentiments.* This, for Meisner, would become the entry point and a kind of magic key for actors to make essential connections with other actors onstage – what I have been calling *transaction*. He even found it more useful than *emotional memory* in getting to *surrender*. That the authentic expression of emotion was as important to Meisner as it was to Strasberg is revealed in a story he liked to tell about a performance by Eleanora Duse, witnessed and reviewed by George Bernard Shaw:

> *... in a play called* Magda. *There's a scene in the last act. When she's a young girl she has an affair with a guy from the same village, and she has a child by him. Twenty-five years later, or thereabouts, she comes back to visit her family who live in this town, and her ex-lover comes to call on her. She accepts his flowers – I got this from Shaw – and they sit and talk. All of a sudden she realizes that she's blushing, and it gets so bad that she drops her head and hides her face in embarrassment. Now that's a piece of realistic acting! And Shaw confesses to a*

> *certain professional curiosity as to whether it happens every time she plays the part. It doesn't. But that blush is the epitome of living truthfully under imaginary circumstances, which is my definition of good acting. That blush came out of her.* She was a genius!

Meisner came to the conclusion that what was preventing actors from accessing their emotions was the intellect. In his book, *On Acting* (yes, the same title as Olivier's book) he

Sanford Meisner

describes his dissatisfaction with the improvisation exercises that had been done in the Group Theater: "These were general verbalizations of what we thought was an approximation of our situation in the play. We were retelling what we remembered of the story of the play using our own words. I came to the realization that this was all intellectual nonsense."

And then he devises a solution to the problem:

> *I decided I wanted an exercise for actors where there is no intellectuality. I wanted to eliminate all that 'head' work, to take away all the mental manipulation and get to where the impulses come from. And I began with the premise that if I repeat what I hear you saying, my head is not working, I am listening, and there is absolute elimination of the brain. If you say, 'Your glasses are dirty,' and I say, 'My glasses are dirty,' and you say, 'Yes, your glasses are dirty,' there is no intellectuality in that.*

And thus was born the *repetition exercise.*

In an article titled, *Acting on and off: Sanford Meisner Reconsidered*, Kim Durham illuminates the apparent tension between Stanislavski's emphasis on action, which requires deliberate activation of the *will* of the actor (number 9 on the chart), and the kind of non-thinking, intuitive process Meisner hoped to foster through the repetition exercise:

> *The movement in Stanislavski's own thought and praxis was steadily towards a stressing of the primacy of action. The position that he finally reached, the method of physical actions, involved a process by which character would be developed through an active exploration of deliberate activity. ... Individual actions may arise spontaneously and without pre-planning, but they are essentially acts of volition directed towards the achievement of particular active desires.*

In other words, the actor's selection of actions broken down into beats is a conscious activity. This type of overt technique might do for the stage, but a more subtle technique is needed for the close-up scrutiny of the camera. Durham references a book on screen acting by the blacklisted Hollywood director Edward Dmytryk, for whom:

> *...the most important signifier in screen performance discourse is involuntary. Without intention, it arises within the actor as the actor is exposed to stimuli. It is not willed by the actor: it happens to the actor. ... The construction of such singularity cannot arise from a fresh exercising of will alone. Rather it depends, at least in part, upon a habit of intense attention to the present reality and a degree of submission to the affective nature of external stimuli.*

This might explain why film director Sidney Pollack was such a fierce proponent of the Meisner technique, even donating his time and equipment to filming a Master Class.

Meisner's exercises were designed to "bridge the gap between Stanislavskian *will* and the revelation of the unwilled spontaneous reaction" to get the actor past the conscious mechanics of action and intention. The repetition exercise uncouples the actor from the demands of a specific text with precise actions and objectives. As actors repeat back to each other simple observations that surface in the moment, "Your glasses are dirty, ... My glasses are dirty, ... Yes, your glasses are dirty" a merging of sense and sensibility occurs as the exercise unleashes the unconscious response.

But repetition tends to hit a kind of ceiling in its effectiveness as a technique. The moment-to-moment spontaneity of the repetition exercise in simple exchanges becomes difficult to sustain during scene work where the actors have specific actions to perform and objectives to accomplish. Meisner would insist that the dynamic of the repetition be maintained even as the demands of the scene grow more complex. To do otherwise would be to revert to the kind of Stanislavskian improvisation practiced in the Group Theater and already rejected by Meisner as "intellectual nonsense." This sets up a problem for the actor/student desperately trying to please the teacher:

> *It is significant that here the student, rather than concentrating on playing the truth of the situation, is monitoring his responses in respect of their suitability to the exercise. ... He suppresses the impulse that arises from his own objective, because it may not meet the approval of the teacher. (Durham)*

This problem with the Meisner technique (at least as diagnosed by Durham) seems to have been solved – or perhaps ignored – by David Mamet and company in *A Practical Handbook for the Actor,* which gives equal weight to *action* and *transaction.*

David Mamet

There is a quality of straightforwardness in *A Practical Handbook* for the Actor that is enormously appealing as it insistently demystifies the craft of acting. Its authors, Melissa Bruder, Lee Michael Cohn, Mad-

David Mamet

eleine Olnek, Nathaniel Pollack, Robert Previtio, and Scott Zigler, studied with Mamet at NYU and were instrumental in the founding of the Atlantic Theater Company, which has since expanded to form the Atlantic Acting School. Despite the long list of authors in which the name "David Mamet" does not appear, it is probably fair to say that the *Handbook* speaks in Mamet's voice as channeled by his students. The current website for the school lists Mamet as a founder.

Mamet sidesteps Meisner's admonitions to banish the brain, instructing the actor to focus on those things that are controllable – her voice, her body, the text as it is given to her, adjustments that the director adds, the action in the scene as she understands it – and to ignore everything else. For Mamet, *action and transaction* trump everything else. *Shape* is simply part of the given circumstances. If the part calls for an accent or a limp, bring it. *Surrender* (emotion) is to be ignored. You cannot control it so leave it alone. According to this technique, if you are working at accomplishing a clearly defined action and your focus is on the *other* (whether that other is a scene partner or, in direct address, the audience) the emotion will take care of itself. It will come.

Well, maybe.

A third element central to the Mamet technique is also one of Stanislavski's tent poles: *Will* (9 on the chart). In the *Handbook* we read: "The only talent you need to act is a talent for working." In other words, anyone can act if she has the will to do so and anyone who says she wants to but doesn't have the knack for it suffers from a lack of will, not a lack of talent. In the opening pages of the *Handbook* the word *will* appears seven times.

87

In other writings Mamet derides most of the teachings of the various studios, workshops and drama departments as "hogwash" and observes (contradicting himself) that the success of many of their students is probably more the result of accident and natural talent than anything learned in an institution. In his book *True and False: Heresy and Common Sense for the Actor*, he observes, "…it is as if Corsica, claiming Napoleon, recommended herself as a training ground for emperors."

For Mamet there is no such thing as *character*. Just the words on the page that will, if you say them clearly guided by a strong, simple *action*, create the illusion of character in the minds of the audience. This is a rather startling and disconcerting revelation for the actor accustomed to preparing for a role by investigating and researching the "back story" of the character, asking questions about the character's history and motivations and then attempting to build a bridge between the character's experiences and his own. Mamet rejects all that work as unnecessary and even harmful.

Much of what Mamet says makes sense. His prescriptions are actable. We can see the results of this approach in the work of his best actors, especially William H. Macy, Felicity Huffman, Joe Mantegna, and Lindsay Crouse. One of my favorite Mamet films is *House of Games* despite the almost parodic quality of some of the scenes. As the actors deliver their dialogue in the ultra-flat, staccato style that is

William H. Macy

his trademark, we can sense his controlling presence behind the camera watching for any sign of the actors breaking away from his stern advisories. Of course Macy's recent work in the Showtime series, *Shameless*, is a riot of over-the-top *shape* play while, at the same time, sounding the occasional note of deeply felt, utter desperation.

Mamet's synthesis of Meisner and Stanislavski is brilliant. He takes the essential piece from Stanislavski – giving the actor a strong, actable *action* to perform onstage – and marries it to a Meisnerian *transaction*, "the test of the action must be in the other person." This simple technique places the actor's attention outside of himself, which goes a long way toward eliminating self-consciousness. Mamet's ability to bridge the divide may be attributable to the fact that, like Shakespeare, he is a fully rounded theater creator; director, writer, and former actor. But he too easily dismisses *shape* and *surrender*. It's true that Joe Mantegna playing a Chicago mob guy is not going to have to do much work to get the shape of that character, but Mantegna will have to do some research, perhaps take some dancing and elocution lessons, when we cast him as a nobleman in the court of Louis XVI.

I agree that the actor is ill advised to play an emotional state, but it's too easy to say, "play the action and the emotion will come." Most of us have built up too many layers of emotional armor. We will need to cultivate a capacity for shedding those layers that buffer us from the existential dread. In order to do that we may need to dip into the *surrender* techniques of Strasberg and Batson. We also need to take the notion of action deeper than the catalogue of verbs offered by Mamet and the book, *Actions: The Actors' Thesaurus* by Marina Calderone and Maggie Lloyd-Williams, which lists more than 150 pages of actionable words such as *Ambush, Beguile, Charm, Demolish… Wound, Yoke,* and *Zap.* We must identify the central action of every character as the construction and defense of the heroic narrative.

FIVE

BEYOND STANISLAVSKI: THE POSTMODERNS

Judging from the approaches to the art and craft of acting we have looked at so far, it almost seems an article of faith that the actor's goal must be the creation of "truth" on stage. The Neighborhood Playhouse states such a mission on the homepage of its current website, where it defines the goal of the Meisner technique: "To live truthfully under given imaginary circumstances." However, at least since Treplev cried out for "new forms" in *The Seagull*, artists have been straining against the movement towards naturalism and so-called "truth" in the theater. It may be that something more than truth is needed. Susan Sontag challenges this assumption of truth as the prime mover of all artistic endeavors in her essay on Simone Weill:

Perhaps there are certain ages which do not need truth as much as they need a deepening of the sense of reality, a widening of the imagination. I, for one, do not doubt that the sane view of the world is the true one. But is that what is always wanted, truth? The need for truth is not constant; no more than is the need for repose. An idea which is a distortion may

Susan Sontag

> *have a greater intellectual thrust than the*
> *truth; it may better serve the needs of the*
> *spirit, which vary. The truth is balance, but*
> *the opposite of truth, which is unbalance,*
> *may not be a lie.*

The postmodern aesthetic deliberately strives to peel back the "truth" presented in culturally constructed buffers, exposing the chaos underneath. No longer is theater (or any other literary form) simply about representing different flavors of *denial* as it manifests in various characters. In other words, it is not serving up a smorgasbord of *shape* choices: the hardworking construction worker struggling to pay the bills; the young ballerina striving to make her mark. Instead, theater now functions as a splash of cold water in the face. It unplugs us from a fabrication of reality that is more virtual than authentic to show us as we truly are: "…no more significant or enduring than cockroaches or cucumbers."

The mentors described up to this point worked primarily as teachers of acting and inventors of systems. Now we shift to other figures recognized more for their output as artists, writers, and directors and whose approaches to acting are more a byproduct of that work. This postmodern phase is a directors' theater in which the actor is often secondary to more dominant stage elements: spectacle, design, and mise en scène. In a review of Richard Foreman's production of *Idiot Savant*, *New York Times* reviewer Ben Brantley neatly, if uncharitably, characterized the postmodern actor/director relationship: "They are stylish robots, carrying out the commands of a dictatorial auteur. People don't so much act in Mr. Foreman's productions… as take orders, the better to embody their director's convoluted currents of thought."

Antonin Artaud

In his 1932 manifesto, later published as *The Theater and Its Double*, Antonin Artaud derided what he felt was the misguided emphasis on realism in the theater of his day by asking, "Whoever said that theater was created to analyze a character? ...such preoccupation with personal problems disgusts me." As he contemplated a Europe already shattered by one World War and about to be drawn into another, theater that mirrored life in the comfortable drawing rooms of a well-fed elite seemed utterly irrelevant to him. He railed against "culture" incapable of addressing empty bellies, and instead demanded

Antonin Artaud

newly imagined theatrical forms that might be as essential as food. The role of artists in such a world should not be "mere recording organisms" but "like victims burnt at the stake, signaling through the flames."

He went on to expound a "theater of cruelty" that would wrench the audience away from the quotidian, and toward a face-to-face encounter with the most elemental forces of existence. Even the use of normal language was, for him, too constraining. Instead he suggested "a vocabulary of gesture and mime for every circumstance of life..." declaring it necessary to "reinstate the worth of theatrical conventions." Artaud was greatly moved by performances of the Balinese Theater. Though performed in a language he could not understand, he found the ancient theatrical tradition so powerful, it moved him to conclude that language was somehow superfluous:

> *Dialogue – a thing written and spoken – does not belong specifically to the stage. It belongs to books... I say that the stage is a concrete physical space which asks to be filled, and to be given its own concrete language to speak... This concrete physical language to which I refer is truly theatrical*

93

only to the degree that the thoughts it expresses are beyond the reach of the spoken language.

Theater makers have drawn inspiration from Artaud's vision ever since. His writings have inspired a host of artists including Peter Brook, Andre Gregory, Blanka Ziska, and especially Jerzy Grotowski, whose appraisal of Artaud in *Towards a Poor Theater* is probably the best we have. In a chapter devoted to Artaud he first lambasts the pseudo avant-garde imposters who, at best, could manage only a superficial impersonation: "...chaotic, aborted works, full of so-called cruelty which would not scare a child..." Grotowski cuts through the mystique built up around Artaud, gently identifying his inaccuracies and shortcomings, while pinpointing his strengths and true greatness. For instance, he pointed out that Artaud's supposed innovations in staging – an audience placed in the center with the action taking place all around – had already been tried by late 19th and early 20th century innovators, Max Reinhart, Meyerhold and Vakhtangov.

Artaud's proposed new theatrical vocabulary of gestural hieroglyphs and "10,000 expressions of the face" is uncomfortably similar to the Delsarte system which, as we have seen, quickly devolved to a catalogue of stale conventions. However, Artaud can and should be forgiven for not knowing what his predecessors had discovered. He came by his insights honestly and independently, just as multiple inventors might have solved the problems of manned flight, the internal combustion engine, or incandescent lighting.

Unlike Delsarte or Stanislavski, Artaud "left no concrete technique behind him, indicated no method. He left visions, metaphors." His essential howl: *wake up!* demands that we strip ourselves bare of the identities and buffers that protect us from true knowledge of the abyss. He challenges us to invent a new theater that might allow us to engage in what Grotowski called *total act,* and which I name *surrender.*

Bertolt Brecht

Tracing the bloodlines of current postmodernists is neither simple nor direct. In relation to the Stanislavski family tree, we might think of Meyerhold and Artaud as genetic mutations spawning entirely different lines that run parallel with Stanislavski. Around the same time that Meyerhold was separating himself from the Moscow Art Theater, a new style of edgy, satirical,

Bertolt Brecht

and decidedly non-naturalistic theater was emerging in the underground cabarets of Munich and Berlin. The theatrical style Bertolt Brecht embraced and expanded would be heavily influenced by cabaret performers such as Karl Valentin, with whom he collaborated.

In addition to being a playwright, director, and critic, Brecht was a prolific theorist striving to make sense of the art and craft of theater making. In *Brecht on Theatre: The Development of an Aesthetic,* he reminds us that whatever verisimilitude we might try to create, we are always in the theater and we'd do better to acknowledge that fact. "The aim of this technique, known as the alienating effect, was to make the spectator adopt an attitude of inquiry and criticism in his approach to the incident." Brecht describes a new kind of theater, where:

> *... stage and auditorium must be purged of everything "magical" and that no "hypnotic tensions" should be set up.... The audience was not "worked up" by a display of temperament or "swept away" by acting with tautened muscles; in short, no attempt was made to put it in a trance and give it the illusion of watching an ordinary unrehearsed event... the audience's tendency to plunge into such illusions has to be checked by specific artistic means....*

95

Gone is the assumption that we want the audience to enter into the illusion of a reality being presented onstage:

> *It is of course necessary to drop the assumption that there is a fourth wall cutting the audience off from the stage and the consequent illusion that the stage action is taking place in reality and without an audience. ...*

Gone too is identification with characters:

> *It is well known that contact between audience and stage is normally made on the basis of empathy. Conventional actors devote their efforts so exclusively to bringing about this psychological operation that they may be said to see it as the principal aim of their art... the technique which produces an A[alienation]-effect is the exact opposite of that which aims at empathy....*

Several new conventions are introduced:

> *Given this absence of total transformation in the acting there are three aids which may help to alienate the actions and remarks of the characters being portrayed:*
>> *Transposition into the third person.*
>> *Transposition into the past.*
>> *Speaking the stage directions out loud.*

Brecht isn't interested in an acting style that will allow the audience to identify with the actor but rather in one that will jar them. He even suggests that the whole concept of the professional actor is unnecessary. His actor behaves:

> *...just as any normal person with no particular acting talent would... if he wanted to portray someone else, i.e., show how he behaves. This showing of other people's behavior happens time and again in ordinary life (witnesses of an accident demonstrating to newcomers how the victim behaved, a facetious person imitating a friend's walk, etc.).*

Thus, with one stroke, Brecht does away with the entire notion of an acting profession, let alone a technique. Ultimately Brecht is most focused on *action*: Characters like Mother Courage, or Shen Te/Shui Ta in *Good Woman of Szechwan*, all have clearly defined heroic narratives, and Brecht shows us what they will *do* in extreme circumstances. *Transaction* is also common, especially as a synonym for negotiation. Brecht deliberately employs flat *shapes*, stock characters, to convey the universality of his themes. He tells us that he does not want *surrender* or catharsis in his plays. If the audience can have their emotions purged in the theater there will no longer be a need for them to take *action* outside the theater–which is what he most wants. Despite that aesthetic distancing and ideological stance, Brecht's works often do succeed in engaging our emotions.

Grotowski

In the 1960s the theater world came to know Jerzy Grotowski, Polish wunderkind, actor, director, leader of the Laboratory Theater, and inventor of a technique he named *Total Act*. He made his directorial debut in 1958, two years after the death of Brecht. The two have often been linked – they both grew up in countries under totalitarian siege

Jerzy Grotowski

97

and developed new forms of theater that challenged established convention.

Somewhat ironically, Grotowski began his career hoping to become an authority on Stanislavski. But Stanislavski, like Anton Chekhov, was part of the cultural elite, a rarified stratum of Russian society that lived in the shade of the aristocracy. Grotowski's world had just survived Auschwitz. *The Cherry Orchard* was much too small and polite for his theater. His actors needed to roar and howl at the outrages of humanity. To do that they would need to strip absolutely bare, emotionally and physically. *Total Act* means total *surrender*. It's also almost entirely anti-intellectual. Recalling Diderot, there's no *sense* in it. Grotowski, like Meisner, didn't want his actors to think. *Total Act* is total sensibility.

Grotowski found inspiration in actor training from the Peking Opera, Indian Kathakali and Japanese Noh theatre:

> *Here, everything is concentrated on the ripening of the actor which is expressed by a tension towards the extreme, by a complete stripping down, by the laying bare of one's own intimity – all this without the least trace of egotism or self-enjoyment. The actor makes a total gift of himself.*

Well, he had me right up to the part about "without the least trace of... self-enjoyment."

Grotowski's seminal work, *Towards a Poor Theater,* charts a course of training and preparation for the actor that verges on the monastic. He worked with actor Ryszard Cieslak for more than a year on his performance of the title role in *The Constant Prince,* which debuted in 1967. His admiration for highly ritualized Asian theatrical traditions, as well as for Delsarte and Meyerhold, suggests an intensely shape-oriented approach to the theater, but the heart and soul of his technique was *Total Act*. This technique required a trancelike, egoless expression that, in its purest form, would be spontaneous and nonintellectual. In other words, completely *surrendered.*

In an article for the *Journal of Religion and Theatre,* "Theoretical Foundations of Grotowski's Total Act," Jennifer Lavy distinguishes between Diderot who "...wants an actor who will 'play [the part] so well that you think he is the person.' With this, he introduces another layer of the paradox: the problem of the actor being himself and simultaneously not himself–presenting a lie of self." Whereas for Grotowski, "Our response to the actor is a total one [that] does not distinguish easily between the actor as a personality and the role he is playing." Grotowski seems to embrace the Meisnerian transactional principle, although he names the *spectator* rather than the scene partner as the *other.* Lavy describes how Grotowski proposes as a goal:

> *...the crux of an actor's art through which one reveals oneself completely to another (the spectator) in a self-reflexive act that does not distinguish between character and self. In total act, Grotowski articulates a dialogical encounter with the spectator in metaphysical terms, which can be difficult to trace out without it seeming as though the sole purpose has become religion.*

The director André Gregory studied, worked, and became lifelong friends with Grotowski. Much of the film, *My Dinner with Andre,* is devoted to his recounting of these experiences. Given the centrality of *total act* to Grotowski's philosophy, I wondered if he had explicitly considered *action* itself as an element worth exploring. After Gregory began summering on

André Gregory

Cape Cod and joined my theater's board of directors, I took the opportunity to ask him about this. In our conversation he said

Well, neither Grotowski nor I really believed in the notion of objective. Let's say you decide to take a train to New York. You might think that your objective in going is to get a job in publishing. But there's a much deeper objective that you aren't really conscious of. You might not truly understand your objective for 20 years.

In a way, Gregory sidestepped the question of *action* when he used the word *objective*, for whatever objective the train traveler might have, intended or not, his *action* – the thing he *does* – is to get on the train. Yet in his answer I heard confirmation of the idea that action goes very deep. The immediate objective might be to "get to New York, get the job," but the deeper, underlying action will be about reaffirming the heroic narrative. This might be the "20 years later" epiphany alluded to by Gregory.

Grotowski's *shapes* are stripped down to the bone. His actors often appear to be rather emaciated and wearing little more than loin cloths. His *transactions* are with what he calls the *spectator. Surrender* would, perhaps, have been the final cause of any Grotowski project.

Robert Wilson

Robert Wilson carries the notion of the "dictatorial auteur" guiding "stylish robots" to an extreme. In Arthur Holmberg's *The Theatre of Robert Wilson*, Seth Goldstein describes his 1985 experience as an actor in *the CIVIL warS: a tree is best measured when it is down* at the American Repertory Theater:

Robert Wilson

> *...every movement from the moment I walked onto the platform until I left ... was choreographed to the second. During the scene at table all I did was count movements. All I thought about was timing. Bob didn't talk about family dynamics or subtext. Nevertheless, from all these different actors counting different movements, a highly emotional portrait of a family emerged that was never explicitly discussed by the director.*

Yet Wilson considered himself to be acutely attuned to the actor's process: "When I look at an actor I have to think about not only the character he's playing but also the person breathing in front of me. I don't like thinking in the abstract. I have to see something to know what I'm doing."

Wilson's background is unusual for a stage and opera director. Originally from Waco, Texas, he studied business administration at the University of Texas before moving to New York, where he received a BFA in Architecture at the Pratt Institute and later studied painting. It is not surprising then that he should focus most on the formal, scenic elements of production. It is also not surprising that he would meet with resistance from some actors. Here's Marianne Hoppe on acting in *King Lear*:

> *This Wilson can't fool me. I started out at the Deutsches Theater with Max Rheinhardt. I know what a director is. Wilson is not a director. He's a lighting designer. A Wilson actor runs here and there only because there's a change in the lights. On a Wilson stage, light pushes the actors around. Light is important, but in Shakespeare, language is also important. I can speak these lines the way he wants, but I don't believe Shakespeare wrote the part of Lear to be recited by an autistic child.*

Others would find freedom in Wilson's method. The French film actor Isabelle Huppert tells of her experience working with Wilson on *Orlando* in Lucerne and Paris in 1993:

> *Usually I prefer the screen. The camera zooms in for a close-up, and like a microscope, it sees into your soul. In theatre you have to be much more exterior, projecting to a large auditorium. But Bob has found a way to capture interiority on stage.... By breaking the conventions of all that exaggerated emoting, Bob has created a new way of acting, a new way of inhabiting the stage that for the first time enabled me to reach the same level of sensitivity and interiority as in film.*

The uber-control of counting and precise movements that drove others mad struck Huppert differently:

> *At first learning all those precisely choreographed movements was difficult, but when I had them down pat and understood how they express Virginia Woolf's novel on a deep level a big surprise came.... Never on a stage have I been so free, so much myself. I felt like a child, playing at home in an attic, all alone. When you think no one is looking, you do the most extravagant things. Bob gives you permission to do this.*

Wilson's approach is perhaps best suited to his own concoctions, such as *CIVIL wars*. There he can work in pure forms, movement, sound, and light, with the actors constituting only one of many formal elements. When it comes to interpreting something as dense in text-driven meaning as a *King Lear*, however, some critics have found the emperor to be without clothes. In *To All Appearances: Ideology And Performance*, Herbert Blau says:

...there was ... the sort of affectless imagism that, however masterful it may have been before, was simply unmastered by the language of the text, whose emotional power is such that, even if minimally spoken, the drama is still there, struggling to appear.... This in turn affected the nature and requirements of the performance, in which the actors seemed confused. The double bind was that there had to be sufficient acting, or enough acting ... to verify the presence of the drama ...once we were reminded, through the spoken words, of the potential capacities of the play, ... no irruption of spectacle, however momentarily imaginative, could overcome the fact that the enactment was rather feeble.

Overlie, Bogart, and the Six (Nine?) Viewpoints

We began with Aristotle's narrowing down of necessary theatrical elements to six. Diderot focused on the Cartesian mind/body dualism in pursuit of the proper balance between passion (which we often associate with "the gut") and a ruling intelligence. Delsarte codified an actor's technique into dozens of poses and gestures. Stanislavski's system, according to Stella Adler's chart, listed more than forty distinct elements. The Stanislavski descendants tried to make sense of it all by narrowing down to one or more essentials: action for Bobby Lewis, *transaction* for Meisner, *imagination* for Adler, *surrender* for Strasberg. The postmoderns walked away from "truth" to get to a non-naturalistic theatrical style, drawing on ritualized forms and trancelike states of egoless surrender. In another part of the postmodern landscape we find the Viewpoints of Mary Overlie. She, like Aristotle, arrived at six essential elements. Beyond that coincidence there is little similarity between the two systems.

Here she describes her origins:

I was born in Montana, began studying dance in a painting studio in Bozeman and worked in summer theater until I was seventeen. From 1964 to 1970 I studied modern dance in San Francisco and briefly worked with the SF Mime Troup. I arrived in NY in January 1970 and became involved with the Judson Church choreographers, Yvonne Rainer,

Mary Overlie

Barbara Dilley and Steve Paxton, forming a company called the Natural History of the American Dancer. I later created the idea of Movement Research and then co-initiated Danspace at St Marks church. In 1978 I became the first faculty of the new Experimental Theater Wing at Tisch School of the Arts NYU. The Viewpoints were first conceived of in Montana using the history of technical development of painting vocabulary as inspiration. The philosophy and practices began to take form in the mid 70's within the minimal conceptualism in SOHO.

Like Aristotle, Diderot, Delsarte, and Stanislavski, she was driven to articulate a system for the creation of her art. From her website:

> *... to conceive of the idea that theater had a basic working language and that I could find it if I kept looking. Eventually I found The Six Viewpoints. The Viewpoints process reduces performance to a code. This code acts like a flexible measuring device much like a transit and rod used in surveying for mapping land. The Viewpoints, like the transit and rod were devised to reveal structure. The structure we see through The Viewpoints is made in six basic windows of perception that are used to create and view theater.*

Overlie's Viewpoints are *Space, Shape, Time, Emotion, Movement,* and *Story.* (She often uses the mnemonic, "SSTEMS –as in stems, or a strange way to spell systems.")

Although she describes the Viewpoints as tools to "create and view theater," their origin in her experience as a dancer/choreographer seems plain. Her use of the term Shape refers to the physical shapes that a dancer would create with the body, as opposed to the way in which I have used it to describe character formed by culture.

Early in her career Anne Bogart collaborated with Overlie and has used the Viewpoints extensively in her work ever since, expanding their number from six to nine. The full list now reads: *tempo, duration, kinesthetic response, repetition, shape, gesture, architecture, spatial relationship,* and *topography*. Much of Bogart's work has also been choreographic, and, like Overlie's, her Viewpoints seem to dwell on the outer manifestations of expression (shape.) Significantly, *emotion* is absent from Bogart's list, causing Overlie to remark, "How could any real theater or dance person take a theory about those forms seriously when it discounts emotion as an element of performance?" There is a deliberate walking away from the Stanislavski tradition in Bogart's approach. In her book, *The Viewpoints Book: A Practical Guide to Viewpoints and Composition* she laments the "…misunderstanding, misappropriation and miniaturization of the Stanislavski system…."

Like Stanislavski's system, Bogart's *Viewpoints* function as an extraordinarily comprehensive curriculum for training actors and developing works of theater. The four essential elements I keep returning to are all to be found in *The Viewpoints Book* (co-authored with Tina Landau). *Action*, certainly. *Shape*, in spades! Their word for *transaction is relationship*, and they delineate five distinct categories of possible *listeners* in a Meisnerian interaction. They describe emotion,

Anne Bogart

105

the possibility of finding and expressing it, as "…a state of aliveness, receptivity and experience." That is as good a way as any to describe a state in which the psychological armor has been dropped, allowing for the possibility of *surrender*.

I studied with Bogart at the American Repertory Theatre Institute during the time she was developing Calderón's, *Life Is a Dream*. (Tina Landau was my classmate.) The exercises were liberating, and the work created was compelling. The aspect of her approach that most interested me as a director was the way in which she would enlist the ensemble in the rehearsal process. Her term for this is *Composition*, "…the act of writing as a group."

In rehearsal, groups of three or four actors would be sent off on assignments to work on mini-sections of the play or even something as specific as a gesture to express a particular moment. After an hour they would reassemble to present their work. The process generated a profusion of ideas, many of which would find their way into the finished product, which was intensely choreographed, dense with movement and gesture. It was a revelation for me, at the time, to discover that the director does not have to generate all the ideas! Still, it's hard not to conclude that the actor is something of a secondary player in an Anne Bogart creation. Like Robert Wilson she dominates the production with her ideas, her choreography, and her mise en scène which is full of gesture and strong forms. My impression, however, is that her actors have more fun than Wilson's.

Some mainstream critics have come to embrace the post-modernist aesthetic. By 2013 Ben Brantley (who still seems baffled by the work of Anne Bogart and Joanne Akalaitas) was greeting a new Foreman production, *Old-Fashioned Prostitutes (A True Romance)*, with:

> *Hello again, Richard Foreman. It's been four years since the last time you walked out on us, leaving us with nothing but memories of intimate nights too crazy to be true. But in our hearts we knew you couldn't quit us….*

*Welcome back, Mr. Foreman. It's kind of
reassuring to know that some 40 years on,
you still have the power to disorient us.*

In this brief history of systems and approaches I have tried
to maintain the elevation and speed of a helicopter – not too
low, not too fast – so that we might gather enough detail to
make sense of it, but also stay above the treetops, so to speak,
in order to appreciate the landscape as a whole. My purpose in
taking this deepish dive into theater history has been to tease
out the commonalities among the various systems, and to find,
if possible, some common ground upon which they all stand.
How, for instance, are we to reconcile the stagey bombast of
the old-school Shakespeareans with the hyper-realism of the
Methodists; the vivid stage imagery of a Robert Wilson with
the performer who yearns to be more than a "stylish robot?"

I don't mean to suggest that such a reconciliation is
not already underway. There are many examples of superb
performances by artists who manage to infuse their bold
shape choices with deeply felt, authentic human emotion, and whose connection with their fellow actors is
complete. These qualities are apparent in the best work
of Fiona Shaw, David Patrick Kelly, Simon Russell Beal,
Pedro Pascal, Brenda Withers, Phillip Seymour Hoffman,
Alfre Woodard, Joaquin Phoenix, Robert Kropf, David
Strathairn, Angela Bassett, and Bobby Canavale. Where
we tend to come up short is in our attempts to verbalize
just what makes these performers great, too often falling
back on cliché and vague euphemism like "natural talent"
and "unknowable gift." We may need a new vocabulary as
much as we need a new approach to the craft.

What I have been searching for, and believe I have
discovered, is a "theory of everything" for the theater. My
theory, reduced to the sort of pseudo-mathematical language employed by Meyerhold (see page 57), might read:

Performance = Shape + Action +
Transaction + Surrender

Take one of the elements away and the equation falls apart.

I use the word "discovered," but none of these four elements are new: Aristotle's most important element, *plot*, might appear, at first, to be purely dramaturgical – the concern of the playwright and not the actor. But plot is the "arrangement of the incidents," and *incident*, in this context, equals *action*. Aristotle's #2 is *character* which is my *shape*. We might consider *spectacle* mainly the realm of the director, but in the hands of the right actor, a spectacular shape – De Niro's Jake LaMotta, Daniel Day Lewis's Lincoln, Streep's Thatcher – is a mighty tool. *Catharsis* – which Aristotle did not include in his "important" six – is my absolutely essential *surrender*. I could go on connecting the dots to every one of Aristotle's findings but you get the point.

Diderot's *sense*, or intelligence, implies all of the head work that goes into researching the culture, history, ethnography, socio-political context – *shape* – of the character. His sensibility is just shorthand for passion – *surrender*. But Diderot had not yet come to *transaction*. We would need Meisner to help us with that discovery. Meisner and Strasberg were both too narrow-focused on the elements they considered key. I've already flogged Strasberg enough for his obsession with *surrender;* "Everything was secondary to it..." noted Clurman.

Recognizing the narrowness of systems like the Method suggests how an actor might use the four elements as a framework for approaching the part in a more comprehensive way.The actor working with a Robert Wilson, Anne Bogart, or some other *shape* driven auteur, might bring their own understanding of *action, transaction*, and (perhaps most importantly) *surrender*, to the work. Likewise, the actor trying to make sense of direction that is somehow all over the place might use the four elements as a manageable anchor. To be blunt, a complete performance requires all four of these elements. To go a step

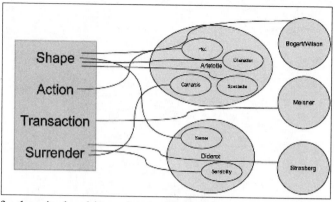

further, it should require nothing else.

In order to support the above audacious claim, I will now devote the next four chapters to a thorough exploration of each of the four elements. I will also show how each of them relates back to, and is supported by, the existential framework.

PART III

The Four Elements

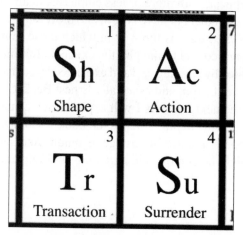

In surveying the many different solutions to the challenge of creating and interpreting believable human characters offered by theater theorists and practitioners since Aristotle, my aim has been to show how some practitioners dealt with the enormous complexity of the actor's task and narrowed it – systematized it – in a way that would render it more manageable. Some systems, like those devised by Delsarte and Stanislavski, included dozens, even scores of elements – too many. Others, like Strasberg and Meisner, resolved to only one – too few. Too many for what? Too few for what? The followers of any of these systems would surely protest that they were *not* too narrow or too broad but, rather, "holistic."

I pose the question in pursuit of unraveling this conundrum: The actor is standing in the wings ready to go on stage. At that moment, if she has "done the work," there are weeks, perhaps months of rehearsal and study that have allowed her to store an encyclopedia-sized trove of information in mental and muscle memory: lines, blocking, cues, relationships, character history, dramaturgy, etc. The question now is, what is the actor to focus on as she steps onto the stage? What is she to *do*? That is what I mean when I say that Stanislavski's chart of elements or even the 6 Viewpoints are "too many."

The four elements that I find to be essential – *shape, action, transaction,* and *surrender* – are not new. They appear and reappear, with more or less emphasis, in all the systems described. What I believe is new, and the reason for this book – its *final cause* – is the way in which those four elements are supported and unified by the existential framework first articulated by Kierkegaard and expanded by so many including Sartre, Lifton, and especially Ernest Becker.

In the next chapters I will explore each of the four elements in some depth. Later in the book I will describe how they cohere in a useful onstage technique and suggest how they might be deployed in a training environment.

W^e all crave meaning, a sense that our lives have purpose and that we are integral members of a larger community that itself has meaning and purpose. Our need for meaning is just an extension of our need for survival – what we must have in order to live. According to Abraham Maslow's famous pyramid, once we have secured the most basic needs – air, water, food, clothing, shelter – we can begin to focus on the less tangible but no less essential need for meaning. As psychologist Robert J. Lifton once put it, "we not only need to live but to feel that we are alive." It is that feeling of aliveness that membership in a culture provides.

When we are firmly enmeshed in a culture, the anxiety brought on by death awareness recedes into the background, since immortality, symbolic or literal, is now on offer via an array of possible heroic narratives. In the next chapter I will explore how, in theatrical terms, the construction and defense of that narrative – that shape – becomes the central *action* that we all share. We all share that common action. The shape the heroic narrative takes, however, is infinitely variable.

Shape is the word I use to describe how a character appears to the outside world. But to think of shape as merely superficial – a mask – is to miss its complex underpinnings. The way we walk, talk, and gesture; the clothing we wear; the way we style our hair and makeup all derive from the cultures we inhabit and are only the outermost expressions of identity. Each culture provides a roadmap, a rulebook, an instruction manual, for individuals within that culture. When we adopt a particular *shape* and sign onto the rulebook, the implicit contract is that if we live by those rules and follow that roadmap, life will have meaning and we shall be granted at least symbolic immortality.

The Big Picture

The stakes couldn't be higher when it comes to the shapes we inherit or adopt. How high? Life and death high. Shape is how we announce our tribal affiliations to the world. The wrong shape in the wrong place can get you killed. This is because the standards and guideposts for one particular culture may not make much sense in the context of another. Shakespeare may have been first (as usual) to nail this down. In *As You Like It*, the fool Touchstone mocks Corin, the old shepherd, for his lack of manners, suggesting that he would flounder at court, but Corin retorts:

> *Not a whit, Touchstone: those that are good manners at the court are as ridiculous in the country as the behavior of the country is most mockable at the court.*

Within a given culture, a person may be honored and respected for certain attributes; perhaps the ability to track an animal and throw a spear with such accuracy that the animal dies instantly. At a cocktail party on the Upper East Side of Manhattan that same individual would find himself utterly unprepared for a different set of rituals. Of course the reverse is also true.

It isn't necessary to choose an example quite so extreme to illustrate the point. Anyone who has experienced middle school may recall the shame of appearing in the not-quite-right uniform and paying for the transgression. More critically, showing up in the wrong Chicago or Los Angeles neighborhood wearing the wrong colors can get you into serious trouble. There are too many examples, historical and contemporary, of life-and-death conflicts between warring cultures: Shia and Sunni, Catholic and Protestant, Hutu and Tootsi, Bloods and Crips. Even when the conflict is legitimately about control of scarce resources, ideology and worldview allow combatants to demonize and dehumanize the *other*, often paving the way for horrific vio-

Austrians Executing Serbs, 1917

lence. In the theater we talk a lot about *raising the stakes*. It may be useful to remind ourselves that people in the real world are literally killing each other over these differences.

Shape in the Real World

After biology has had its way with us (genetics do much of the work of determining our shapes) *character* is formed from the outside in. We can only know who and what we are from the feedback we receive from the outside. Beginning in the womb and progressing through infancy, childhood, adolescence, and adulthood, at each stage we receive vital information from parents, siblings, peers, teachers, communities, and the media about what shape we might adopt. All of it goes into the choices we make in forming the heroic narrative – the *causa sui* project.

Causa sui is Latin for "cause of itself." At the heart of the existential framework is the notion that we willfully choose our identity with no help from fate or God. As I will explore more fully in the next chapter, Sartre's notion of shape choice, *existence precedes essence*, strikes me as too absolutist. We do have options for what we might become, but those choices are constrained by the culture in which we find ourselves. In an earlier time, shape was more static and predetermined; the son of a bricklayer was likely to become a bricklayer himself. Nowadays the son of a stockbroker may choose to become a painter, but he is unlikely to wind up hunting and gathering in the bush. Today we are bombarded with images suggesting that anyone might become wealthy and famous by pursuing a career in professional sports or show business. The chances of this actually happening may be slim, but that does not prevent many from going after those glittering shapes.

There is nothing static about shape. Over the course of a lifetime we are likely to adopt and subsequently slough off numerous identities. Robert J. Lifton wrote about the historical progression from static to fluid identity in his book, *The Protean Self:*

Robert J. Lifton

For most of our existence we have been embedded in immediate relationships and functions... one behaved in certain ways toward the people around one, according to status, role or occupation, and geographic place. One did so because one was required to (would be shamed and punished if one did not) and because one wished to (had internalized these requirements and made them one's own).

But times have changed:

The symbol systems have by no means disappeared, but they have become less effectively internalized, more a matter of external requirement. Hence, there is a loss of a sense of fit between what individuals feel themselves to be, and what society or culture, formally or informally, expects them to be.

Today we make more conscious decisions about our heroic narratives, leaving room to change our minds – and careers – repeatedly. The self-styled poet switches majors and transitions to something more "realistic," only to rediscover her artistic side later in life and turn, perhaps, to painting.

Once formed, shape must be defended. It is inherently fragile, susceptible to challenge, and always a work in progress. In the very young it presents itself as a multitude of possibilities. Adults ask children, "what do you want to be when you grow up?" The frequency with which the question is posed probably reveals more about the insecurities and preoccupations of the adults than it does the children being asked. Nevertheless, it is the central question for us all.

Riding the bus or the subway we see shape in all its glory. Mostly we see examples of people "wearing the standard uniforms – but allowing themselves to stick out, ever so safely, with a little ribbon or a red boutonniere, but not with head and shoulders." Wherever we look we see examples of people who have signed up as members of different tribes that are all somehow nestled within the larger American culture. The uniforms may be off the rack: Brooks Brothers, or The Gap, or Macy's. The morning rush hour is dense with suits, but closer examination reveals the infinite variations of shoes and ties, cut and color. We also see marvelous examples of shape gone wild. In our culture, Becker's "little ribbon or a red boutonniere" becomes a tattoo, a piercing, dreadlocks, or purple hair. I always enjoy observing people who look as if they're starring in their own movie.

Shape in Fictional Characters

When we look at literary and dramatic characters through the existential lens, we see that the crisis of the central character often hinges on the success or failure of the *causa sui* project. As the story begins, the heroic narrative of the character is well under way; the shape is set. Then something happens to disrupt the narrative. The assumptions that went into that narrative and that shape are suddenly questioned, perhaps shattered. What follows is a journey towards either restoring the narrative or finding a new one.

As we track the following examples, remember how high the stakes are when it comes to identity. If the heroic narrative allows us to believe we are valued members of an ordered and meaningful universe and that our participation in a given culture provides us with a sense of literal or symbolic immortality, the demolition of that narrative means we no longer have a buffer between ourselves and the full force of death anxiety. Suddenly our lives have no more meaning than a speck of sand or a bug. We are reduced to a mass of quivering protoplasm. We will do almost anything to protect or restore the integrity of that buffer.

Hamlet: Young prince Hamlet is firmly embedded in a culture of wealth and privilege. He is a college student surrounded by good friends and poised to inherit a crown and a kingdom. This narrative is interrupted by news that his father has died and his mother will soon marry his uncle. The disruption is amplified by the appearance of his father's ghost, who charges him to avenge the murder. Cancel the kegger at Wittenburg.

Oscar Wilde

Wit: A brilliant professor, Dr. Vivian Bearing is secure in her intellect and her profession. Her shape is defined by her brilliance, her ability to use language, her power over her students and her colleagues. Then she learns that she has cancer. Margaret Edson's play charts the steady stripping away of all those identity defining elements. Vivian's existence is literally threatened, but it is the loss of her sense of self that is even more wrenching – for her and for us.

The Importance of Being Earnest: demonstrates how even the most frothy comedy of manners is driven by existential motivations. What does it mean to be "Earnest"? The play abounds with questions of identity and tortured shapes (corsets anyone?). Lady Bracknell bears an edifice of armor signifying centuries of calcified cultural buffers. She is the walking, talking embodiment of the cultural code. The more seriously the actress (or actor!) playing her takes that mission, the funnier the performance is likely to be.

The Great Gatsby: Jay Gatz, born in poverty but mindful that his inherited shape might not be carved in stone, literally reshapes himself as Gatsby. The persona he constructs – owner of fast cars, beautiful shirts, a mansion with staff, and hordes of admirers – can be undone all too easily by a Tom Buchanan. Tom may be a boor, but Gatsby understands that, compared with Tom, he will never be more than a pretender. Gatsby's real weakness is Daisy, who represents the most glittering prize of all. His endless need to merge with her precipitates the actions that lead to his doom.

Stuck in Shape or Shape Shifting?

If shape is the outer manifestation of psychological armor, that shape, if it's interesting, can be an actor's entrée to a career. Indeed, one of Stella Adler's injunctions to her students was "don't be boring!" We may talk about a John Travolta or Danny De Vito *type*, but that shape can become a trap that prevents the actor's career from blossoming. Career stagnation may stem from a lack of imagination on the part of directors and casting directors but it may also be an indication that the actor's own character armor has calcified into a particular shape he or she is unable or unwilling to break through.

Some of the most memorable and celebrated performances have been defined by the performer's ability and commitment to shape *shifting*. Famous examples include Robert De Niro's Jake Lomotta in *Raging Bull*, Dustin Hoffman as Ratso Rizzo in *Midnight Cowboy*, and Ben Kingsley or Daniel Day Lewis in just about anything. We rarely hear about a Meryl Streep type, because she seems to shift shape for every role.

The Iron Lady

Much of Meryl Streep's physical transformation into Margaret Thatcher in *The Iron Lady* is attributable to her makeup artist, but that only goes so far. The performance is built on layers of shape elements: language, dialect, posture and bearing, the way she walks, and the way each of these evolves as she gets older – all are Streep's creation. The importance of shape is even woven into the narrative of the film; to give Thatcher a more commanding presence her handlers deliberately alter her hairdo and engage a vocal coach to deepen and strengthen her voice.

Meryl Streep

The film's final shot begins with Streep as Thatcher sitting at a table drinking tea. She carefully sets the cup down as if in recognition that there is the possibility of miscalculation in the act of doing so. She rises, first placing her feet deliberately beneath her and both hands on the edge of the table to support her weight. She moves to the sink with the cup and saucer. Responding to her assistant's inquiry as to whether they might visit the House of Lords she replies, "No, no. I'm not going anywhere." Yet we see that she is perfectly dressed in a trim grey suit, pearl necklace and earrings, with a matching brooch pinned to her lapel. Her hair is coiffed, lipstick applied. She scrubs out the cup in the sink, then turns and walks away from the camera. She carefully navigates her way past a chair, allowing one hand to linger on its back until the last possible moment, then moves down the hall, feet slightly splayed, back slightly bowed. Her gait is slow and shuffling yet purposeful.

Behind each of these physical choices is a wealth of personal and, more importantly, cultural history. Culture is the fertile ground from which all shape choices grow. The culture from which Thatcher arises is British, middle class, and male dominated. *The Iron Lady* makes a great case study because it chronicles Thatcher's progression from girlhood to adulthood. We see how she is shaped by her love and admiration for her father. "Grocer's daughter," an epithet used against her, becomes a point of pride. She inherits his ramrod bearing, his fierce conservative convictions, and his belief that success is achieved through hard work. It is in this context that her identity is forged. Her sense of purpose and her sense of herself as a heroic figure drive her throughout her life (and Streep throughout the film). Her heroic project takes a very specific shape, one defined by country, community, family, political orientation, fashion, hairstyle, accent, and, later, physical and mental infirmity.

The brilliance of Streep's performance is that it does not come off as a superficial impersonation. She has soaked up all the cultural DNA available to her, identified the central driving action of the woman, and woven it all together into a coherent and convincing whole.

Cindy Sherman

No one has explored the expression of shape more fully than the performance artist/photographer Cindy Sherman. She has built an entire career around assuming different identities and then photographing herself in meticulously staged environments. Except for a decade-long period when she stepped out of the frame and constructed grotesque collages using props and mannequins, this has been the focus of her entire body of work.

Cindy Sherman

Through her deep investigation of shape, Sherman also manages to incorporate *action, transaction,* and *surrender.* Working alone in her studio (she employs no assistants and functions simultaneously as photographer, stylist, art director, and subject), she enters into a transaction with the viewer, implicitly asking us to validate the causa sui project on display. Using costume, makeup, props, and es-

121

pecially her facial expression, body posture, and gesture, she manages to suggest an entire narrative that the viewer is invited to construct along with her. What imbues many of her images with such urgency is that the figures are often captured in the act of defending identity projects in the final stages of decay and collapse.

The Fallacy of the "Magic If"

The actor who takes on a role in which the shape of the character is very different from her own may ask, "How do I get inside the head and under the skin of this character whose experience is so distant from my own?" The answer provided in conventional acting training often involves some combination of *imagination and substitution.* Invoking Stanislavski, we are told to employ the *magic if,* as in, "What *if* you were a serial killer?" or, "What *if* you were the king of England?"

In *An Actor Prepares,* Stanislavski begins the chapter titled *Imagination* with, "You know now that our work on a play begins with the use of *if* as a lever to lift us out of everyday life onto the plane of the imagination." In *The Stanislavski System,* Sonia Moore tries to explain what the master meant: "This 'magic *if*' ... transforms the character's aim into the actor's. It is a strong stimulus to inner and physical actions." *Imagination* was also a central element in the teaching of Stella Adler. In fact, the following appears on the current website of the Stella Adler School of Acting:

> Actors' imaginations are the most powerful source for them to draw on.... students at the Stella Adler Studio are asked to use their imagination to locate the fullest range of motivational force, rather than depending solely on their personal past and emotional memory.

Is this useful? I believe that the notion of the actor using his imagination to enter into the world of the character, which by now is conventional wisdom and a core value of the Stanislavski family tree, is due for reconsideration. Ricky Gervais, with Ian McKellen as willing co-conspirator, brilliantly sends up the *imagination* trope on an episode of his show, *Extras*. Gervais' character has achieved some success starring in a sit-com but has decided that what he really needs is the credibility that will come from acting in a play. He learns that Sir Ian is directing a project and manages to land an interview. Sitting across from Gervais at a table (sycophantic assistants hovering in the background), Sir Ian peruses Gervais' resume and murmurs, "Not much theater work of late." Then, without warning or setup, he launches into the following dissertation on acting technique:

> *Sir Ian: How do I act so well? (pregnant pause) What I do is, I pretend to be the person I'm portraying in the film or play.*
> *Gervais: Yeah...*
> *Sir Ian: You're confused...*
> *Gervais: No...*
> *Sir Ian: Perfectly simple - case in point:* Lord of the Rings. *Peter Jackson comes from New Zealand, says to me "I want you to be Gandalf, the wizard," and I say to him, "You are aware that I am not really a wizard," and he said, "Yes, I am aware of that. What I want you to do is to use your acting skills to portray... a wizard... for the duration of the film." So I said, "Ok," and then I said to myself, "how would I do that?" And this is what I do. I imagine what it would be like to be a wizard... and then... I pretend it. I act it, in that way, on the day.*
> *Gervais: Yeah...*

Throughout the exchange Sir Ian is speaking in the most earnest tones as if he is imparting some incredibly profound, hitherto unrevealed knowledge. Gervais stares back at him with "what am I missing" bewilderment, conveying to the audience that what Sir Ian is saying is the most obvious thing in the world. I love this vignette because it also happens to capture – and puncture – the mystique that so often accompanies the transmission of knowledge from acting teacher to student.

Of course acting is pretending, but we need something more organic, more visceral, and ultimately simpler that will allow us to inhabit our characters in a truly believable way. When the underlying action of a character – any character under any circumstances – is the same as the underlying action we engage in all the time, we no longer need to construct artificial bridges between ourselves and the characters we are playing. We no longer need to imagine or pretend. We simply need to *be*.

This idea has enormous ramifications. Hannibal Lecter's heroic narrative includes killing people and eating them. Lady Macbeth and Richard III are willing to commit unspeakable acts to get what they want. When we use *imagination* to get into the heads of these characters we are really distancing ourselves from them. That act of distancing carries the danger of rendering the performance artificial. Lecter, Lady M, and Richard are doing what we all do – defending the heroic narrative in order to feel whole, to achieve symbolic immortality by fulfilling the rules – no matter how perverse – of the worldview they have adopted.

When we consider shape separately from the other elements, we can begin to utilize meticulous research and intensive physical work to construct characters that are rich in historical and cultural detail. I suggest that if we restrict ourselves to the *magic if* formulation – "What *if* I were a court jester in Elizabethan England, L.A. gangbanger in 2013, cowboy in the 1800s" etc. – the characters we create will be smaller and less interesting.

Ultimately it is not really possible for me to *what if* myself into the reality of another character whose culture and life experience are so different from my own. What I can do is to suit up in the ***shape*** of that character with as much detail and texture as possible. I can locate the *other* – the transactional figure most important to that character. I can then plunge into the transactions mandated by the script carrying *my own* action of defending the *causa sui* project.

The real work is to know what it feels like to construct and defend our own heroic narrative. We need to be centered in our own *causa sui* project and experience the life-and-death struggle to assert the viability of that project in every transaction of our lives. This is part of the important *work on one's self* Stanislavski placed at the number one position on his chart.

SEVEN

ACTION

We now understand that shape functions as a buffer and bulwark against the anxiety brought on by death awareness. This means that the viability of that shape is a matter of the greatest urgency – life and death actually – because a failure of that project of identity would trigger a deep psychic loss, an unacceptable failure of meaning and purpose for the character. Indeed it would trigger such a loss for ourselves if our own shape was shattered.

In our historical survey of the different approaches to the art and craft of acting, action is ubiquitous. It comes up again and again as an essential focus of the actor's concentration. So why revisit this most common of arrows in the actor's quiver? What is not different here is the notion that we choose actions to help us focus on what we want to accomplish in a scene. What is different, and may be startling for some, is my assertion that all characters share the bedrock action of constructing and defending a heroic narrative.

Motivation, Intention, Objective, Action

In rehearsal we ask, "What is the action for the character in this moment?" This appears to be a rephrasing of the cliché, "what's my motivation?" The word *action* needs unpacking, though, because embedded within it are the concepts of *motivation, intention,* and *objective.* Although they are often used interchangeably, they really mean very different things.

A person may be motivated by hunger. If so, his objective or intention will be to satisfy that hunger. His actions might be to beg, borrow, barter, seduce, steal, kill, or otherwise acquire food. In practise, we might use the word *action* as shorthand for the whole process. *Action*, however, is not what we desire (motivation) or what we intend (objective) but what we *do* to satisfy desire and intention.

The fuse is lit. The clock is ticking. The hero races to defuse the bomb before it goes off. This most fundamental action – to survive – may help explain the durable success of the Hollywood action blockbuster. If someone holds a pillow over your face your action in that moment is immediate and clear: remove pillow; reestablish conditions conducive to breathing. But humans require more than just being alive (and, perhaps, more subtle fictional narratives). Once the basics of life support are in place – food, clothing, shelter – the hunting and gathering begins for that most essential human commodity: *meaning*.

Abraham Maslow charted this brilliantly with his "hierarchy of needs" pyramid which has since entered the canon of psychological theory. Maslow's pyramid, starts with literal survival (air, water, food) and rises through layers of progressively enhanced symbolic survival. Yes, we need shelter, but we seem to aspire to more and more square footage, manicured lawns, Sub-Zero® refrigerators, and Viking® stoves.

Such objects are really talismans conferring meaning within the context of the culture: different cultures, different talismans. Culture reassures us that the world we live in is stable, orderly, and meaningful. It then instructs us in how we should exist within that world. We are offered an array of templates or roles by which we might fashion a heroic narrative. The successful construction and maintenance of that project affirms that we are valued members of an ordered and meaningful universe. Once our physiological needs have been met, accomplishing this successfully becomes the central and most crucial of human actions.

For the major characters in *The Iliad*, survival itself appears to be almost secondary to establishing that they have lived and died in accordance with the Greek code of honor. For Shakespeare's Julius Caesar, infallibility is so central to his sense of self that in the run-up to his assassination he will ignore all warnings. He would rather die than show the weakness any wavering might communicate to his subjects. In *The Pillowman*, by Martin McDonagh, the writer Katurian Katurian is so invested in his sense of himself as *writer* that he bargains relentlessly with his interrogators to ensure the preservation of his stories after his impending execution. Once he secures that promise he is able to greet death with something like aplomb. Each of these characters is engaged in the *action* of defending their heroic narrative.

Sartre

In his essay, *Existentialism is a Humanism*, Jean Paul Sartre pronounced that *"existence precedes essence,"* arguing that it is only by our actions that we define the essence of our existence:

> ...*man will only attain existence when he is what he purposes to be. Not, however, what he*

may wish to be. ...I may wish to join a party, to write a book or to marry. [But] there is no love apart from the deeds of love; no potentiality of love other than that which is manifested in loving; there is no genius other than that which is expressed in works of art.

In other words, what we might imagine, or hope, or wish for, or even plan is almost irrelevant compared with what we *do*. Thinking about art does not constitute making art. We "attain existence" when we choose specific actions that define the essence of that existence. The essence/dianoia/final cause of a man is revealed in his actions. Man chooses to act in contrast to objects whose *"essence precedes existence."*

Sartre offers the example of a letter opener that "...has been made by an artisan who had a conception of it." The need to open a letter efficiently (or cut the pages of a book) calls into existence the idea of a letter opener whose purpose is to open letters.

Man, according to Sartre, comes into existence essentially blank. He exists but he

Jean Paul Sartre

does not yet have essence. He does not have *shape* in the culturally constructed sense, nor has he yet chosen or begun to construct a heroic narrative. "Man simply is.... Man is nothing else but that which he makes of himself. That is the first principle of existentialism." For Sartre, *action* is what elevates man. He is more than simply an object whose essence has been preordained, even by a creator. "Man is, before all else, something which propels itself towards a future and is aware that it is doing so. Man is, indeed, a project which possesses a subjective life, instead of being a kind of moss, or a fungus or a cauliflower."

Or a letter opener.

The beauty – and the curse – of existential man is that he has the freedom to choose his identity. We are reminded of Kierkegaard's *angst* – joy and terror embodied in the same breathtaking moment of awareness of an existence that must end: "Thus, the first effect of existentialism is that it puts every man in possession of himself as he is, and places the entire responsibility for his existence squarely upon his own shoulders."

Kenneth Burke

Man is *causa sui* – he creates himself. Where I part company with Sartre is in my belief that none of us is able to wholly create ourselves. We enter the world as we might enter a crowded room. Within that room we find *culture*, and it is that culture that offers up various templates – *shapes* – for the *causa sui* project.

Language as Symbolic Action

Just as Ernest Becker worked to construct a "Science of Man" – a broad theory that might answer fundamental questions about what makes us human and what makes us act the way we do – so did the literary theorist Kenneth Burke, who came at it from a different angle. According to Burke what separates man from other animals is the way we use symbols, especially language. "Man is the symbol–using (symbol making, symbol–misusing) animal...." Language for Burke is a *symbolic action system*. In other words, the very act of speaking is an expression of the heroic narrative. The actor stands on stage and must speak (even occasionally without

Robert Kropf
in *Love Song* at WHAT

131

words) to accomplish some action, especially the primal action of reinforcing the *causa sui* project. We have in common with our characters our fundamental need to express action in language.

As a director I have frequently encountered actors who found it difficult to project. One of the most distasteful instructions we can demand of an actor is "louder!" so we struggle to rephrase or euphemize that simple command in a multitude of ways. It is rare that the actor is physically incapable of speaking louder; rather that doing so feels artificial. Somehow volume and "truth" seem incompatible. Method actors have sometimes been accused of "mumbling." This technical defect surely comes at least in part from the actor struggling to look within for that deep connection to the character being created. Patsy Rodenburg calls this tendency *first circle*, "...an inward moving, drawing energy towards the self."

What I suspect is really going on has something to do with heroism in the deep sense that Ernest Becker writes about so eloquently. It is surely heroic to stand before an audience and assert the right to be watched and listened to. But when we dare to be heroes and assert that we have cosmic specialness, when we dare to *speak* in defense of that existence, we make ourselves susceptible to the other feeling: that we are, in fact, insignificant specks of dust in an indifferent cosmos. Therein lies the true definition of stage fright. No wonder that we have difficulty speaking up and out under those circumstances.

When the act of speaking is understood to be an *action* in and of itself, strong projection usually follows as a matter of course. "I speak therefore I am!" might be a good way of thinking about it. Becker said, "The most that any one of us can seem to do is to fashion something–an object or ourselves–and drop it into the confusion, make an offering of it, so to speak, to the life force." In the chaos and confusion that is our fully perceived universe an authentic action will be to contribute something, "an object or ourselves" – or a work of art in the form of the spoken word.

The Artist's Action

For most of us the causa sui project takes the shape of a vocation or identification with some group. For the artist the causa sui project may be bound up in a sequence of personal experiences that take a certain shape (bohemian attire?) and form a heroic narrative. But the artist's central project is located in the art object that is outside the self. Otto Rank, who was first a disciple and then broke with Freud, described this phenomenon in his book, Art and Artist. Ernest Becker does the hard work of synthesizing and paraphrasing Rank's dense treatise in the following passage:

Otto Rank

> *The work of art is, then, the ideal answer of the creative type to the problem of existence as he takes it in – not only the existence of the external world, but especially his own: who he is as a painfully separate person with nothing shared to lean on. He has to answer to the burden of his extreme individuation, his so painful isolation. He wants to know how to earn immortality as a result of his own unique gifts. His creative work is at the same time the expression of his heroism and the justification of it. It is his 'private religion' – as Rank put it. Its uniqueness gives him personal immortality. ... (Becker)*

The artist fashions the work of art in response to the "problem" of existence. The universe is chaotic, meaningless. To survive we *must* find meaning within that chaos. For many of us that sense of meaning comes from our identification as part of a group, as a member of a family,

133

as a productive worker or a skilled technician. The artist imagines something that does not yet exist: a story to be told, a painting or sculpture; for the director, a play that, so far, exists only as a blueprint in the form of a script; for the actor, a character that so far exists only on the page. In our imagination we can see the finished art object – perfect, brilliant. But then we go to work to create that object, that performance, and start to worry:

> *What right do you have to play God? Especially if your work is great, absolutely new and different. You wonder where to get authority for introducing new meanings into the world, the strength to bear it. Your very work accuses you; it makes you feel inferior. It all boils down to this: the work of art is the artist's attempt to justify his heroism objectively, in the concrete creation. It is the testimonial to his absolute uniqueness and heroic transcendence. But the artist is still a creature and he can feel it more intensely than anyone else. In other words, he knows that the work is he, therefore "bad," ephemeral, potentially meaningless—unless justified from outside himself and outside itself. (Becker)*

This goes far to explain the syndrome of the "tortured artist" for whom the work is never good enough, never finished. At a certain point all one can do is walk away, stop editing and correcting and begin another piece. The remarkable film, *The Mystery of Picasso*, shows the artist painting on a piece of glass with the camera looking through from the other side. We witness a storm of creativity as one seemingly perfect creation after another is painted over and destroyed, giving way to another and then another. A perfect example of the never-satisfied artist.

I was fortunate to assist Andrei Şerban on a production of *The Miser* at the American Repertory Theater. In rehearsal he was tireless, meticulous, inventive, ever changing and adjusting. I was startled to learn that he was known for never attending his opening nights. It was as if he could not bear to see the "finished" work that, for him, could never be truly finished, could never hope to attain the perfection he saw in his mind's eye.

Another artist with whom I've had the pleasure of collaborating is Dan Joy who, for 18 years, was resident set designer at Wellfleet Harbor Actors Theater. As we worked together I was sometimes frustrated by the way he seemed to never be quite finished with a set. There was always a better prop to swap out, a bit more set dressing to add, paint to touch up.

Dan Joy in *Goose and Tom Tom* at WHAT

This quality has always defined, for me, the difference between the artist and the hack. The hack can be satisfied with the art object. The true artist never is. When we combine this inability to be satisfied with that other essential quality – the willingness and ability to remain open and vulnerable to the truth of our mortal insignificance – we begin to understand how difficult it can be to be an artist and why so many of the truly gifted ones lead such excruciatingly difficult lives.

When There Is No Heroic Narrative

If antimatter is the opposite of matter, we might imagine something like *antiaction* to describe certain characters and conditions that seem to defy everything stated so far about how characters respond to death awareness. The premise has been that we and the characters we portray respond to the anxiety induced by death awareness by constructing heroic narratives that provide a sense of purpose and literal or symbolic immortality. But what are we to make of characters like Georg Büchner's Woyzeck, David Mamet's Edmond, James

Dean's Jett in the film *Giant*, or Hedda Gabler? These are characters who, when confronted with a world in which they seem to have no place, react by destroying everything in sight as they plunge into the abyss. There is nothing conventionally heroic in their actions which seem designed only to hasten a rendezvous with chaos and death. Fortunately the un-heroic actions of the antiheroes are as supremely watchable as they are actable. The current landscape of film and TV is crowded with these characters.

Breaking Bad's Walter White learns he is dying of cancer and decides to parlay his knowledge of chemistry into a lucrative new career as a crystal meth cooker and dealer. His ostensible motivation and nominal *action* in doing so is to provide a comfortable financial cushion for his family. But as the series unfolds over the course of four seasons it becomes increasingly clear that Walter is driven by deeper impulses than making money. He has, in fact, made so much of it that he requires a rental locker to store the bricks of cash – millions – he is amassing. His literal collision with mortality may be front and center, but story elements emerge that are even more significant than his terminal diagnosis. We learn, for instance, that Walter is a former Nobel prize winner and that, while he languished in obscurity as a high school math teacher, his early scientific discoveries somehow launched a former classmate and business associate into the upper stratospheres of Silicon Valley success. He also suffers the daily humiliation of implicit comparisons with a brother-in-law who is a successful, and unlike him, macho, Federal agent. All these circumstances contribute to a toxic brew of failed *causa sui*. His newly constructed identity as "Heisenberg," the ruthless and brilliant meth lord, proves so intoxicating that he becomes capable of almost anything, including the torture and murder of his adversaries. The potency of his need to triumph in this project of identity is evidenced by his eventual willingness to abandon his wife and son, the supposed beneficiaries of his decision to "break bad."

Don Draper, the protagonist of *Mad Men*, would seem to have it all: the perfect family, a high-powered position in a

Madison Avenue advertising agency, and plenty of money to support a lavish lifestyle, not to mention the charm and devastating good looks he is able to parlay into sexual adventures with a seemingly unending parade of beautiful and willing women. At the core of this "success," however, is emptiness born of a traumatic childhood; raised in a brothel by a prostitute mother and alcoholic pimp father. He also lost his true identity – literally – when he survived a foxhole bombardment in Korea and assumed the name and privileged past of his dead comrade. Don's own self-destructive behavior – alcoholism, compulsive womanizing – can be seen as desperate attempts to create an authentic sense of self where now there is only an empty shell or, at the very least, deaden the pain.

Jon Hamm

In the smallest, seemingly least significant moments of our lives, as well as in the moments that we might recognize as important, we act and are guided by motivating forces that, in the theater, we call *actions*. We can ascribe specific, targeted intentions/motivations/objectives to the smallest of these. Behind them all lurks the overriding action of constructing and defending the *causa sui* project – the project of inventing ourselves in meaning and identity. This project takes a specific *shape*. That shape may morph and change with time. When the shape is temporarily lost or shattered, our most compelling action may be to find our way back to that shape, discover a new one that feels authentic, or, if we lose our way, simply destroy everything in our path.

EIGHT

TRANSACTION

Once we know what our *action* is, the next step is to determine whether we are accomplishing that action. More to the point, we need to identify exactly *who* will let us know that we are accomplishing that action. That there is a who is certain: character is formed from the outside in. We only know who and what we are from the feedback we receive from the outside. The actor/character/person who moves through the world unaware of or unconcerned with the signals he is receiving from other actors/characters/people is, by definition, disconnected, ineffective, and perhaps suffering from a diagnosable personality disorder. Of course, this particular affect can be a legitimate character choice. But even then the *other*, the one from whom we seek validation and with whom we need to transact (perhaps hidden from view and invisible to outside observers), still exists.

For now let's proceed on the basis that, as David Mamet says, "the test is in the other person." Placing attention outside oneself is, at the very least, a valuable tool that helps offset the crippling self-conscious-ness that can afflict an actor. It also fits perfectly with our

Casey Clark and Dan Joy in
Waiting for Godot at WHAT

broad theory about character and character creation. When our primary *action* is to reinforce the heroic narrative or, if that narrative has been shattered, to rebuild or reinvent it, it is essential that we secure validation for that action. We must know where we are in the success or failure of that project.

Identifying the *other* is usually straightforward; for Hamlet it is the Ghost, Gertrude, Ophelia, or the Gravedigger, depending on the scene. For Vladimir it is Estragon – and vice versa. For Willy it is Biff – and vice versa. In each of these pairings we know that the character is invested in a heroic narrative that must be tested in transaction with the other half of the pair.

All of these are high-value relationships – friends, lovers, parents, enemies – and the consequences of the transaction are obvious. But even the most banal interactions, the ones we have with shopkeepers, passing strangers, and acquaintances as well as the minor interactions we have with friends and family, are loaded with meaningful dynamics that help us locate ourselves within the culture we inhabit and signal to us that we are, or are not, accomplishing the *action* of defending the *causa sui* project.

Sociologist Erving Goffman meticulously tracked and studied these seemingly innocuous interactions in his book, *The Presentation of Self In Everyday Life*. Although Goffman's field was sociology, he found the metaphor of performance useful in framing his findings.

Erving Goffman

In the preface he states, "…the perspective employed in this report is that of the theatrical performance; the principles derived are dramaturgical ones…" and goes on to speak of the individual "sustaining his performance" and maintaining "belief in the part one is playing." He makes careful distinctions between persons who genuinely believe in their performances and those who "put on a show" for reasons both cynical and altruistic. The overriding message of Goffman's work is that the ordinary transactions that dominate everyday life are freighted with psychological significance. We *care* about what other people think about us.

Another major figure in psychoanalytic theory, Erik Erikson, also studied the ways in which people rely on the validation of others. In his groundbreaking work, *Child-hood and Society*, he suggested the eight stages of development through which a psychologically healthy person would progress. In Erickson's view the need for validation from the outside, particularly intense in the years from infancy through adolescence, should by adulthood give way to a sense of autonomy and the ability to self-validate. But Erikson acknowledged that a sense of "smallness" persists throughout life:

Erik Erikson

> *Every adult whether he is a follower or a leader, a member of a mass or of an elite, was once a child. He was once small. A sense of smallness forms a substratum in his mind, ineradicably. His triumphs will be measured against this smallness, his defeats will substantiate it. The questions as to who is bigger and who can do or not do this or that, and to whom — these questions fill the adult's inner life far beyond the necessities and the desirabilities which he understands and for which he plans.*

In other words, the essential existential worry that we are insignificant specks of sand in a vast and chaotic universe is too much part of the human condition for us to be able to grow out of. It stays with us and propels our actions in ways large and small. In life we may not be consciously aware that we are acting out the *causa sui* project. Too bad, really. As Becker notes:

> T*he question that becomes then the most important one that man can put to himself is simply this: how conscious is he of what he is doing to earn his feeling of heroism? [It is) the main self-analytic problem of life. ...Everything painful and sobering in what psychoanalytic genius and religious genius have discovered about man revolves around the terror of admitting what one is doing to earn his self-esteem.*

We humans exist in every moment of our lives as players in our own self-created heroic narratives. If we are self-aware we may be conscious of that construct. Being aware of the *causa sui* project may not release us from the demands of fulfilling that project, but it may provide us with enough perspective and irony to prevent us from acting out its most negative consequences.

The actor – the existential actor – does know, *must* know and understand the nature of the character's heroic narrative. We might rephrase the above quotation from Becker in the following way: What is the character doing to earn her self-esteem and what shape does her heroic narrative take? The actor must have the self-awareness that many if not most people are denied. When we become aware of how we move through our own narratives carrying the *action* of constructing and defending the *causa sui* project we have inherited or adopted, we no longer need to build artificial bridges to the *action* of the character; *they are one.*

The importance of placing attention on the other as we test the validity of our actions in the myriad transactions that take place in the lives of ourselves and our characters was reinforced when I came across a reference to the German word *achtung* in a book by the artist/philosopher Adrian Piper. Piper noted that Immanuel Kant considered *achtung, (respectful attention)* something close to a high moral ideal in the context of how people communicate and interact with one another:

> *And when Kant says that Achtung impairs 'self-love,' he does not mean that Achtung crushes our egos or makes us feel ashamed of being the self-absorbed worms we know we are. He means, rather, that the value, significance, and power of the thing that compels our attention compels it so completely that we momentarily forget the constantly clamoring needs, demands and egocentric absorptions of the self; the object of our respectful attention overwhelms and silences them. For that moment we are mutually absorbed in the object of contemplation, or in actively responding to it ... rather than trying to mine the discussion for transient satisfactions of our psychological cravings for self-aggrandizement.*

Adrian Piper

Piper writes at length (and with some humor) about the vicious world of academic philosophy, where intellectual bullies eviscerate one another in subtle and not-so-subtle ways. *Achtung* in this context represents "the intellectual attitude involved in [the] moral virtue of high civilization" that she feels is sorely lacking in current academia.

I find the above passage from Piper compelling in its relevance to the experience of being onstage and *paying respectful attention* to what is happening outside of us. When we commit to *achtung* we are both fulfilling our primary ac-

143

tion and engaging in a process that can help us alleviate the self-consciousness that is the actor's worst enemy.

Patsy Rodenburg

In a system she calls, "The Three Circles," Patsy Rodenburg puts the principal of transaction to work for the actor in a practical way. In her broad theory, in place of the terms transaction or *achtung*, we find *Second Circle*.

Patsy Rodenburg

Rodenburg's first circle is the circle of "self and withdrawal." It represents a way of being in the world that is essentially passive and hiding. The first-circle actor (and person) is neither communicating effectively nor making contact with either the scene partner or the audience. We have trouble hearing the first-circle actor because the energy is falling inward rather than being directed outward. In Beckerian terms, the person who functions in first circle is probably overcome by guilt and dread, afraid to individuate, afraid to assert the heroic narrative.

Third circle is the circle of "bluff and force." Individuals who operate in third circle seem to be attempting to impose their will on those around them. They over-individuate. They don't listen. The outward-directed energy is "…non-specific, and is untargeted. It is as if you are spraying your energy out to the world with an aerosol can."

Neither of these two ways of being in the world is especially effective, either for the person or for the actor. Of course the actor may be called upon to play a character who embodies one of these circles. The ideal for Rodenburg, both for the human being and for the actor, is second circle:

> *In Second Circle, your energy is focused. It moves out toward the object of your attention, touches it, and then receives energy back from it. You are living in a two-way*

*street – you give to and are responsive with
that energy, reacting and communicating
freely. You are in the moment – in the so-
called "zone" – and moment to moment you
give and take. Both giving and taking in that
moment are equal to each other.*

Rodenburg's second circle embodies the essence of the
Meisner repetition exercise, Piper's *achtung*, and of course,
transaction. I attended a three day intensive Shakespeare
workshop with Patsy in order to experience second circle
first hand. Her work with actors focuses mainly on the
fundamentals of freeing the voice and body, the same areas
that might be addressed by a Linklater or Alexander technique. Her approach to the text in Shakespeare is decidedly
non-intellectual; the characters seem always to be working
out their intentions in the act of speaking, very much in the
spirit of *I speak therefore I am.* For Rodenburg "doing the
work" is mostly about tuning up the voice and the body –
and cultivating the ability to do everything from that state
of openness and availability she calls second circle. I found
it enormously useful.

Soliloquies

*Now I am alone. O, what a rogue and peas-
ant slave am I!*

There are two occasions when the actor is "alone"
onstage. The first is called *direct address* and involves the
actor speaking directly to the audience. In that circumstance
the actor will be on the lookout for aural and visual cues
that indicate whether the audience is listening and engaged.
Stand-up comedy lives or dies in this transaction. The other
circumstance, the soliloquy, finds the actor alone on stage
yet, for some reason, speaking out loud – surely one of the
most difficult "realities" to justify.

One good way to justify this behavior is to think of language itself in terms of what Kenneth Burke called *symbolic action*. The act of speaking can be a way, in and of itself, to assert one's existence. Most of us have, at times, engaged in the practice of talking to ourselves. Thoughts are often unwieldy, unformed, spinning off in tangents. Forming thought into speech helps us consolidate those thoughts and render them rational and meaningful.

So with whom are we transacting in the soliloquy? From a technical standpoint the actor can and should be receptive to the aural and visual cues available from the audience. (Coughing and shuffling are telltale signs that the audience is *not* engaged.) But doesn't this take us outside the character and the play? Perhaps, but there is always some level of artifice involved in acting, some balance between the warring sense and sensibility described by Diderot. The ideal may be to lose ourselves in the part and forget everything else, but shutting the audience out entirely and going inward threatens to deliver us to Rodenburg's dreaded first circle.

There are other possible *others* with whom one can transact, whether alone onstage or even with others present. The *other* may be an absent figure from the character's life – a mentor, a parent. It may be a spiritual beacon of some kind – God, or simply a sense of "what's right" – that the character uses as a moral guidepost. In Hamlet's "O, what a rogue" speech it may be that he is in transaction with the dead father who exerts such influence on his actions throughout the play. Hamlet's soliloquys are memorable because in them we hear Hamlet working out *in the moment* just who he is and what he must do. This is one of Shakespeare's great strengths as a writer as well as the key to performing him effectively. The language itself conveys the action of the character and the play.

As we move through our lives (and the journeys of our characters) we look for cues to the success or failure of those actions in the *transactions* between ourselves and other people. It may be that we can only escape from the need to construct heroic narratives and the consequent need to seek validation for those actions from others when we *surrender* to an inescapable truth: all action is ultimately futile, since death is inevitable.

NINE

SURRENDER

All that has dark sounds has duende.' Those dark sounds are the mystery, the roots that cling to the mire that we all know, that we all ignore, but from which comes the very substance of art.... This 'mysterious force that everyone feels and no philosopher has explained' is, in sum, the spirit of the earth, the same duende that scorched Nietzche's heart as he searched for its outer form without finding it, and without seeing that the duende he pursued had leapt from the Greek mysteries to the dancers of Cadiz and the headless Dionysiac scream...

—Federico García Lorca

We know that the earliest plays of Sophocles, Aeschylus, and Euripides were presented in competitive festivals honoring the cult of Dionysus, the god of wine and intoxication. Half mortal, Dionysus was the last god to be accepted at Olympus; he is an outsider and so becomes known as the god of the "other." He represents wild nature, unchecked sexuality, and is often associated with androgyny. "As a god of ecstatic possession, Dionysus left his worshippers without individual, conscious identity; his female followers were called maenads, 'raving women,' and are shown in frenzied, trance-like states."

Sound familiar? Is it too much to name Dionysus the original drama queen? He is the god of letting go, of letting it all hang out. He is the god of *duende*, of *surrender*.

In many ways *surrender* is the most elusive of the four elements. The ability to let go, to experience and communicate authentic emotion onstage, is perhaps the most difficult skill for any performer to develop, no matter what medium an artist works in or what instrument the artist happens to play. An artist might be technically proficient and yet somehow unable to bring real emotion to the performance. Shape, action, and transaction are all attainable through work: An actor with intelligence and

Dancing maenad

a willingness to focus can analyze a scene, determine which action is appropriate in the given circumstances, and then play the scene utilizing those choices. Shape is something we can achieve through diligent research; we can observe and mimic specific physical characteristics, study and perfect dialects. Transaction can be honed through second circle and repetition exercises; the actor who relentlessly focuses outward and learns to listen will become a better actor. *Surrender* requires something different altogether. It is extremely difficult to produce an authentic laugh, or even to smile on command, let alone cry, without *indicating* – that is, fashioning the appearance of the emotion without really feeling it from the inside. The ability to surrender on cue is the holy grail of acting technique.

The capacity to feel and to express authentic emotion is, of course, intrinsic to being human. We begin life without armor. From the moment we leave the womb, life comes at us delivering pain and pleasure that we receive and surrender to in pure expressions of joy, fear, horror, and wonder. We laugh and cry, shout out, sing, giggle, and scream without filter, without self-censorship.

Why do we stop reacting in this way? In a word, *culture*. As Oscar Hammerstein wrote, "You've got to be carefully taught." Gradually over time we armor up. Infants are allowed to mewl and cry and gurgle, but the patience of adults eventually wears thin, and soon we are asking our kids to be quiet. Each culture defines these things in its own way, and permission to surrender is granted differently from one culture to the next. In the west, at least, spontaneous eruptions of any kind tend to be discouraged. Boys learn that it is unmanly to cry. Girls learn what is and is not "appropriate" to express. Gary, a hyper-paranoid character in Laura Mark's play, *Bethany*, rants:

> *They're socializing her. They're teaching her not to hit other kids, and to keep her skirt down, and raise her hand when she has to go to the bathroom. Every single thing her body wants to do is getting smashed down by the military-industrial complex, and the worst part is that it happens all day, every day, to everyone, and everyone just lets it happen.*

Every culture creates these mores according to its own set of rules. Why do cultures impose these buffers? As I wrote in Chapter One, it is a collective response to the cosmic unknowns, the questions that plague all humans: Where do we come from? What are we supposed to do while we're here? Where do we go after we die? Each culture develops its "correct" answers to these questions, and those answers must be inculcated in its members.

In society and in the individual, mortality awareness causes angst. Remember that *angst* does not translate simply as *anxiety*. Angst is both the terror of death and the exhilaration that comes with a full appreciation of *life*. Either of these two conditions, terror *or* exhilaration, is too much for us to live with in every moment of our lives. Terror is paralyzing. Exhilaration makes us do crazy things. We need to dial it back. If our children are acting out, bawling with fear or raving with manic ecstasy, they won't be able to learn much, will they?

We place buffers between ourselves and those feelings.

151

We deny the fact of death through elaborate mythologies whose function is to soften and temper these horrible/amazing realities. The shape we assume as part of a tribe, a family, a community, comes with a massive set of instructions about how we are to behave. We walk like this, talk like this, marry, dance, fight like this. We work at jobs, or study, or make art. We accomplish, or maybe we just hang out. But whatever we do, we do it according to the rulebook. We might decide to reject the rulebook, to choose a different rulebook that is a subset of the subset of the rulebook. None of us wants to be thought of as conforming, so we have our idiosyncrasies. Our hair is short but our sideburns are long.

Every person is the product of cultural conditioning. Likewise, every fictional character exists in the context of a culture – contemporary, historical, or imaginary – and is the product of that cultural conditioning. The artist who creates, interprets, or portrays that character is, of course, also the product of his or her own cultural conditioning. We need to unpack how *surrender* functions for each of these separate entities:

The living human being who is not a character in a fictional work
The fictional character that has been created
The actor whose task it is to portray that fictional character

The human being is living out a heroic narrative shaped by his or her culture, feeling or suppressing feelings according to the circumstances. When events pile up and reach a breaking point, emotions burst through no matter what buffers may be in place. Before it reaches that point we have culturally acceptable releases, escape hatches, that provide us with relatively safe opportunities to surrender. Some of these "living on the edge" activities can get us into real trouble: we get high with drink or drugs, we drive fast, go snowboarding in avalanche zones, have unsafe sex with the wrong people. The flip side of denying death is seeking out more life. Entire industries are founded on this need; amusement parks with "death-defying" rides, whole genres of movies – horror, thriller, slasher – exist to bring us to the edge of oblivion and return us safely to our buffered lives. Children love to play on swings and seesaws and merry-go-rounds, and if they don't have access to any of that equipment they will simply spin around and around and around....

In short, the armor we carry is both essential and unbearable.

The fictional character behaves according to the understanding of its creator and is shaped by the cultural context and construct of the fiction within which it exists. But the fictional narrative is shaped and controlled in a way that life rarely is. As actors we must examine the character through the dramaturgical lens, attempting to divine the intentions of the playwright. Where does the character sit on the continuum from most open and vulnerable – most able to surrender – to most shut down, most heavily armored? Is the character already exposed? Is he written as a truth teller whose

Who's Afraid of
Virginia Woolf

function is to tell it like it is? Or does the playwright introduce truth serums that trigger moments of surrender, allowing the character to escape from his normal inhibitors? In how many plays does alcohol fill that role? Think of the escalating pandemonium in Who's Afraid of Virginia Woolf? as round after round of cocktails are consumed.

What is the inciting event that triggers a shattering of the shape that has buffered the character from awareness of his or her mortality? The protagonist is swimming along in a heroic narrative that is working just fine. Then blam! The established narrative comes apart, the causa sui project fails. The moment when this occurs is often the occasion for the expression of extreme emotion in some form – and it may take unexpected forms. People don't always react to catastrophic events in predictable ways, but they do react. Unless of course they are so heavily armored, so shut down, that they are simply too numb to react at all.

Some characters may be locked in cultural cement and it may be their function in the play to remain so. Willy Loman's neighbor, Charley, aims low, succeeds low, and is perfectly at home in his identity. We won't see Charley express emotions that are in any way extreme. Of course Miller didn't write a play about Charley, but he needs Charley in the play to provide a reference point against which we can measure the other characters – Willy, Biff, Happy – who are pushing against theirshapes, wrestling with their heroic narratives.

The most interesting characters are often tested in such a way that they are forced to surrender at crucial moments in the play. Blanche Dubois arrives at Elysian Fields swaddled in layers of armor the audience can immediately recognize as barely adequate to protect this most vulnerable human being. She erects barricades of clothing, makeup, chatter, and dim light, all in an effort to keep at bay the forces – including her own memories – that constantly threaten to rush in and crush her into nonexistence. One of Stanley's functions in the play is to batter away at Blanche's façade until it comes apart. Stanley himself is a masterpiece of armored male dominance, certainty, mastery, and preening sexuality. But even his armor is shattered when he comes face to face with the prospect of losing Stella, the most important transactional figure in his life.

Nora in *A Doll's House* presents a façade of perfect wife and mother. Her bubble of deceit gets bigger and bigger as she must expand the lies that hold everything in place. Her husband, Torvald, is also carrying around an edifice of pompous, self–created identity: "the bank manager" for whom Nora is the ideal accessory. The tarantella she dances provides the perfect and necessary release of sexual and psychic tension. When Nora's deceptions are revealed, an explosion is triggered that demolishes Torvald's armor and reveals him to be the small-minded, shallow man he truly is. This revelation initiates Nora's catastrophic loss of self. Seeing Torvald revealed, she can no longer sustain the character fictions she has so strenuously maintained throughout the play and throughout her life. With this loss, however, she is free to discover who she might truly become. A new, more authentic heroic narrative will be forged.

The performers, the artists, the practitioners who will be required to interpret and inhabit these characters are at the same time living persons with their own built-in psychological makeup living out their own heroic narratives. These human beings have been raised in specific cultural contexts. Each of them carries culturally constructed psychological armor that protects against death awareness. Each arrives with his or her own shape. The degree to which the actor can bend and transcend that shape will determine how much he or she gets to transcend the typecasting decisions that may be made by directors and casting directors. The actor is the result – perhaps the victim – of the layering up of psychological armor that his or her family, his or her culture, decided was appropriate.

Some artists are lucky enough to have escaped an overly constrictive upbringing. Risking a diagnosis of "oppositional defiant disorder," they might have instinctively rejected the conditioning that was forced on them. They somehow managed to grow into adulthood without being crushed by the cultural judgment of parents, teachers, and peers who tried to force them to layer up the emotional and psychological armor. Some lucky few find it easy to express their feelings, to surrender. Their authentic emotions are available to them. Most of us are not so lucky. Learning to surrender may require a lengthy process of unlearning, unpacking the layers of negativity and shame that prevent us from feeling and expressing those feelings.

Phillip Seymour Hoffman

Maybe "lucky" isn't the right word. Some of our most brilliant artists have had the quality of being so open, so vulnerable, that they ultimately were

155

destroyed – or self-destructed – because of that vulnerability. Marilyn Monroe, James Dean, Montgomery Clift, Janis Joplin, Amy Winehouse, and Phillip Seymour Hoffman come to mind. With tougher skins they might have survived, but they also might not have been nearly as worth watching. The paradox of mental health is that to function in the world we need the layers of armor that protect us from psychic assault, but those layers deaden us and prevent us from feeling. Finding the right balance is akin to a classic engineering problem: Engineers always strive to design an object – a bridge, the wing of an airplane – with just enough strength so that it can withstand extreme forces, but light enough so that it has an aesthetic quality of ease. Too much structure and the thing becomes bulky and coarse; too little and it collapses. It is the actor's obligation to perform a feat of psychological self-engineering, to strip away every layer but that which will allow the actor, the artist, the person, to function in the life space he inhabits away from the stage or the lens. These three entities – the real nonliterary human, the literary invention, the artist/actor/interpreter – may exist on different reality planes, but they are all driven by the same life/death paradigm. All three exist for a reason. They inhabit a heroic narrative, a causa sui project.

As you move through the world you are in a constant state of constructing and defending that narrative. No matter what else you are doing, no matter what other goals you may have, and no matter what other items are on your agenda, this is your primary action. It isn't static; you may wake up one day and decide you want to do something else, be someone else, so you make those changes and move on, and then that becomes your heroic narrative, your shape, and you carry on, constructing and defending that.

Let's pretend for a moment that life is a kind of single-shooter video game. You're moving through the landscape, constructing and defending. How do you know it's working? How do you know this identity project is doing what it's designed to do? You can glance at the shop windows you pass along the street. That tells you the shape is intact. The hair, the clothes, the walk, the smile. But that's not enough. You need other people. The transactions are coming at you fast and furious. People on the street are looking at you or not looking at you, and both of those carry weight. The guy who sells you the newspaper looks up or doesn't, or says hello or doesn't, or seems to smile, or gives you attitude with your change. For some reason it matters. All of these transactions tell you whether the action is succeeding.

Three elements are now in play. The heroic narrative that stands between us and death awareness and that takes a particular shape is in place. Constructing and defending that shape is our action. The validation of that action is tested in every transaction, from the most innocuous to the most essential. There may be those outside the culture whose good opinion we can live without, but from those within our own culture we look for – we need, we demand – that validation to know that existence has meaning and purpose. This dynamic of action defending shape tested by transaction is a machine constantly cranking. It exists within a bubble we count on to remain intact because it contains and protects that sense of surety we call self-esteem. Each transaction builds up or tears down the edifice of self-esteem. When the bubble is shattered we are brought face to face with insignificance, meaninglessness, death, and then the unbuffered howl of the infant is released. How, as artists, as interpreters, can we strip away those layers when the role demands we do so – on cue?

We should begin by accepting that, emotionally, we will not be able to go from zero to sixty. If we move through the world and therefore onto the stage or in front of the lens encased in psychological armor, we will not be able to conjure emotion, even by summoning the memory of a sad or traumatic event. The artist must engage in a conscious daily process of self-examination and stripping away the cultural armor. We need to open ourselves – and stay open – as much as possible. We need to perform that feat of psychological self-engineering that strips away as many layers as possible, leaving only what is necessary to function in the world. When we do we will find that, while we may open ourselves to pain, we also open ourselves to the possibility of greater joy. This is the big work, the life work, to which we must commit ourselves. There are also practical things we can do as we get ready to perform. There is no technique that does not include some kind of preparatory relaxation warm-up. Almost nothing can happen creatively if the mind and body are not in a state of relaxation.

In the 1890s, the Australian actor Frederick Matthias Alexander found himself suddenly crippled by hoarseness. He worked his way through and out of this condition by developing a series of relaxation exercises. His eponymous technique has proliferated wildly ever since. Focusing primarily on body alignment, the Alexander Technique "...shines a light on inefficient habits of movement and patterns of accumulated tension, which interferes with our innate ability to move easily and according to how we are designed." Today there are thousands of certified Alexander teachers worldwide, and the technique

Frederick Matthias Alexander

is taught in colleges and universities as well as in workshops and master classes.

Kristin Linklater has certainly left her mark in the realm of vocal production, with many Linklater-trained teachers at work around the globe. More than 100,000 copies of her highly influential book, Freeing the Natural Voice, have been sold. She too was influenced by Alexander. Both of these techniques aim to eliminate tension from the body. Proponents of Alexander and Linklater would probably not put it quite this way, but I would say that they both offer tools for facilitating

Kristin Linklater

our capacity to surrender. As we strip away the culturally imposed psychological armor that prevents us from expressing what we are feeling, we also need to be mindful of the physical impediments that armor has built up in the instrument. Alexander and Linklater help us knead free those knotted muscles wherever they may be. Music also has a remarkable capacity for fostering a sense of surrender. Music, whether sung, played, or just listened to – and especially combined with dance – creates an almost irresistible opportunity for surrender. Disco, rave, electronica, square dancing, what are these if not excuses for people to bust out of their daily armor and just let go?

Autobiographical digression

The connection between music and surrender was revealed to me many years ago when I was a teenager busking for spare change on the streets of Paris. I had started playing the guitar at the age of ten, and by the time I was in high school I was fully enmeshed in what came to

Me at 12

be known as the "folk revival." For me that meant covering songs recorded by Joan Baez, Pete Seeger, and Bob Dylan. My performance style was strictly first circle; my living room audiences would be required to lean in to actually hear my diffident croonings.

That all changed the summer I traveled to Europe. I was living in a fleabag hotel on the Left Bank and, despite my lousy French, had befriended a bunch of street kids who immediately recognized the franc-generating potential of my guitar. Soon I was standing on the Boulevard Saint-Michel gearing up to deliver my limited repertoire of Motown covers. After a few minutes of losing the battle with traffic, I realized I would have to push past my innate 17-year-old shyness and deliver something I had never before needed

159

and didn't really know I had in me. Then I was belting out Marvin Gaye's, *Can I Get a Witness* and chopping the strings so hard I would end the day with raw fingers. Faces turned, a crowd gathered, and the francs started dropping into the hats of my eager friends. What happened to me as a performer that day was life changing. Pushing past the walls of my armor kicked me into a new zone – surrender. I would never again retreat into a first circle bubble of introversion when I sang. Even back in the living room or in a small club setting, the act of singing for me would mean letting go.

A year or so later, having taken a year off to perform in clubs and coffee houses, I found myself at a tiny liberal arts college in New Hampshire. In 1968 Franconia College was at the center of the counterculture educational revolution, where students were encouraged to "design your own program." It was even stranger, therefore, that the man in charge of the new theater department was a rather old-

Me working with Bennett at Franconia

school autocrat named Ronald Bennett. British, a former member of the Michael Chekhov Company turned Hollywood dialogue coach, Bennett demanded a level of focus and discipline from his students that was completely out of character with the rest of the school. How he landed at hippie haven Franconia is a mystery. That I landed in Ron Bennett's theater department was also not a foregone conclusion. My chosen heroic narrative until that time was "singer-songwriter" and had been since I joined my first band at the age of 14. I entered Franconia as a music major but detoured at the start of the second semester when Bennett recruited me to play Laertes in a production of *Hamlet*.

As I began the transition from one form to another, I was already quite self-aware about the sense of release I had discovered on the streets of Paris. This was my gift, and I hoped to carry that gift with me from singing to acting. It turned out to be much, much more difficult to make that journey than I had imagined. There's something in the act of singing that engages the whole body. The simplicity of a song lyric allows us to flow through the words in a way that speaking dialogue does not. (An exercise often used in Stanislavski/ Method-based acting classes is for the actor to stand alone in front of the class and sing "Happy Birthday.") Theater demands a level of intellectual engagement that takes us out of our bodies and makes it difficult for us to surrender in the way that seems to come easily when we sing. Once I had made the transition from music to theater, I found myself in a world where routine daily activities somehow required rethinking and relearning: how to walk, talk, gesture, inter-act with other people, make myself heard, and, yes, express emotion. I found I needed to "study" how to do these things believably onstage.

The process seems mysterious and esoteric, which may explain why we so willingly submit to the sway of gurus who promise to deliver us unto brilliance. Richard Schechner said of Grotowski, "The tradition he comes from is that of the seer-shaman." Acting technique as worldview creates fierce advocacy in its adherents. An advance copy of this manuscript triggered an angry outburst from some contemporary follow-ers of Delsarte who felt I had not shown sufficient respect for his teachings. It may have that affect on the followers of other one true paths.

There are many existing strategies and techniques for shedding the armor and cultivating the ability to express authentic emotion. Tadashi Suzuki asks us to stamp on the ground. Perhaps in this stamping we are cracking open the armor. Jean-René Toussaint leads work-shops in freeing what he calls the "primitive voice." Grotowski is no longer with us to demand our total act, but others are surely making those leaps into the unknown. Whether we explore

Jean-René Toussaint

traditional psychotherapy, mindfulness meditation, or emotional memory exercises, we would do well to contemplate how the armor we carry buffers us from our fear of life and death. Connecting the dots back to Ernest Becker doesn't make it any easier, but it might provide a conceptual framework that helps us make sense of what we need to do to surrender.

A story told by Patsy Rodenburg beautifully illustrates the power of surrender as it connects the experience of an ordinary human being with a brilliant performer. She describes speaking to a group of mostly actors and artists while on a book tour when she notices "...a little man in a suit, and he didn't seem to be part of the audience. And I started to get very upset because he was very upset." At the end as she is signing books she notices him again. "I saw him hovering over there and I thought, Oh no, I've got to meet this man... and he waited until most of the people had gone and then he came up to me and he said, 'I don't like theater.' And I said 'OK' and he said, 'My wife and I once went to the theater. We didn't like it.'" It seems the man had seen a performance of *The Trojan Women*. Rodenburg asks him why they didn't like it and he says, "'Oh there was this actress... she made a sound. She lost her son.'" "Oh yes, Andromeche," offered Rodenburg. "She loses her child, her young son. He said, 'yeah, yeah... we didn't like her.' But why didn't you like her?" asks Rodenburg. "'She made a sound. It was really embarrassing.'" And then something seems to come over the man. "He got really quiet, and there was a change in his

Aomawa Baker as Andromache in Brad Mays' Production of Euripides' *The Trojan Women* at ARK Theater Company

energy and he looked down to the floor, and he looked up at me, and he said, 'A year ago a policeman came to my door and told me my daughter had been raped and murdered and I made that sound.'" Rodenburg pauses in her retelling of the story and says, "Whoever that actress was, I bless her!"

And we should all bless her. In a moment of unfathomable rage and grief, a horrible sound erupted from the guts of a man in a moment of pure surrender. It was the "dark sound" of Lorca's duende, "from which comes the very substance of art." The actress who is able to unleash a sound like that from a place deep within herself deserves our thanks and our appreciation. The man may not have liked her, but he probably needed her.

TEN

PUTTING IT ALL TOGETHER

In chapter three I spoke of two pathways or phases in actor training, each leading to different outcomes. The preparation phase, encompassing broad avenues of research and investigation, might last a very long time, perhaps a lifetime. Here we explore the text, teasing out every nuance of meaning and context. We also work to perfect the actor's instrument; voice, gesture, movement. This is the big "work on one's self," which is the true legacy of Stanislavski as opposed to the "miniaturized" version of him that has focused disproportionately on emotional and sense memory. This work, however thorough, may deliver the actor to the wings, but it doesn't necessarily help her navigate the performance.

The performance phase requires a completely different set of tools. The essential question posed by Tina Fey, what am I supposed to be thinking about when I'm on stage? demands a much more concentrated focus. In the many possible answers to that question lies the essence of what we call technique. It is what we seek when we sign up for the conservatory, class, or acting coach. The not-so-brief history of theatrical systems and approaches to acting offered in the previous chapters spanned both sides of the equation. Driven by the guiding principle that some reduction is necessary, I conclude that the four elements, shape, action, transaction, and surrender, provide a useful set of tools that bridge both phases.

Two of these elements, shape and surrender, fall squarely in the preparation category. We approach the question of shape scientifically, almost as anthropologists. The character exists in the context of a certain culture, with its own vocabulary of language, accent, gesture, costume, gait, etc. The character has adopted sets of beliefs that may include religious, philosophical, or political stances. All of it functions as a buffer against the existential dread that threatens to rob us of our significance. Successful adherence to the shape definitions provided by the culture provides the character with a sense of meaning, purpose, and yes, literal or symbolic immortality. The rehearsal phase gives us time (hopefully) to fully explore these aspects of the character and embed that shape deep in psychic and muscle memory.

Surrender is not so much something we study as prepare for. Yes, we should study the character from an objective viewpoint, asking whether the character as written is psychologically armored or, instead, open and vulnerable. We can look for those moments in the text when the character's armor is shattered or they suffer some trauma that triggers the release of emotion. We can recognize these moments as occasions when the playwright deliberately signals the actor to bring this element to the performance. But cultivating the capacity to surrender on demand is an ongoing process more akin to the athlete who engages in regular physical conditioning, the musician's daily scales, or the dancer who practices at the barre. The capacity to surrender must be fostered so that when the shape-shattering moment arises onstage the actor is able to deliver the goods.

With surrender and the physical manifestations of shape essentially in the background, the actor is free to focus consciously on just two elements, action and transaction. Script analysis has helped determine specific action choices to accomplish objectives – I want/need this so I will do that. If seduction doesn't work we move on to persuasion and then to bullying. But underlying these specific actions is the one essential action: to construct and defend the project of identity, the shape that embodies not just our own battle with mortality but the battle being fought by the entire culture in which we are embedded.

How do we know whether the action is succeeding? We know it in the transaction that delivers feedback from the outside world. The test is in the other, says David Mamet. We enter the stage in second circle with our attention on the other, watching and listening for signals – from the other actors onstage, from the audience, even from someone or something that isn't present onstage – that will let us know the action is working. That we are whole.

We are all infected with being human. We're all going to die and we all know that. Each of us inhabits a particular culture, and we've either inherited or deliberately chosen a shape that helps us feel that we are at least symbolically immortal. All of us move through the world employing actions that reinforce the sense that the choice we've made, the shape we embody, is a good choice. In the myriad transactions that happen every day of our lives we look for signals that the choice is working. Each of us will suffer traumatic events that shatter the shape and force us to surrender to the emotions flooding in.

The character you play may or may not look the same as you or come from the same culture – it doesn't matter. Work on the shape of the character as a separate problem. That's just research and muscle memory. Costume, makeup, dialect, gesture, gait. Go ahead – consult Delsarte – there might be an attitude of the eyebrow that helps you define that character's shape. Do that work and then forget about it – it's in your muscle memory.

The shape of the character may be different from your own, but whatever it is, your action in every moment of the play is to construct and defend it. And since that's what you have been doing your whole life with your own shape, you don't need to substitute anything. Consider how much psychological armor the character is wearing and whether at some point that armor gets pierced and you've got to show what's underneath. Some characters are totally solid – they never reveal anything – that's ok. Serve the playwright. Some actors try to give their part a moment of surrender no

167

matter what's written just to show they can – don't do that. But if that character is destroyed and you have to show it, remember that you wear armor too. You've got to figure out where your layers come from and how to remove them. Walk on the stage ready to defend the causa sui project to the death. That's what's at stake. And by the way, if it's a comedy it will be funnier when the stakes are a matter of life and death.

Shape is built with research and rehearsal. Surrender is something you'll spend your whole life figuring out how to do, because you've already spent most of your life layering up the armor that prevents you from feeling anything, because that's what we have to do to function in the world. So those two are in the background. You're standing in the wings and you're about to go onstage. You've got that action to pursue – now go out there and work the transactions with whoever it is, real or imaginary, that gets to judge you. That's two things to focus on in the moment of being on stage. Simple.

PART IV

Plays

ELEVEN

DEATH OF A SALESMAN

The Existential Actor is a dramaturgical tool that can be applied to any play or film or, indeed, any fictional narrative. In the next chapters, beginning with *Death of a Salesman*, I will use this tool to explore a number of plays chosen from different periods and genres. Arthur Miller's great American play lends itself beautifully to the existential lens.

In an interview with New York Magazine during rehearsals for his 2012 Broadway revival, Mike Nichols bucked the conventional view of the play as an indictment of the American Dream and declared that it is more about "the need for recognition." But this begs the question of root causes. Yes, Willy, in all his transactions – with Biff, Linda, Ben, Charley, Howard – seeks validation of his chosen heroic narrative. But it is the failure of that narrative, the wrongness of its choosing in the first place, the way it is handed down from one generation to the next and the choices made in accepting or rejecting it that are the true center of the play.

Shape derives from culture, so we begin there. We think of *Death of a Salesman* as a quintessentially American play, but if Miller had not worked so hard to strip out his own roots, it might have come to us as a "Jewish play." Miller wanted Willy to be an Everyman, and he may have decided that in 1949 Everyman could not be Jewish. This stripping out has the effect of rendering the ambient culture of *Death of a Salesman* somewhat bland and colorless. We know we're in Brooklyn, but we get none of the specific ethnic color that might have embellished the language if we could hear the play in Miller's authentic Jewish voice. Instead we get generic catch phrases such as "oh boy" and "don't be a pest" that might have been spoken by any American of that era. This lack of color actually serves Miller's purpose, because he wants the play to speak to a journey common to all Americans – all people really. That he achieved his goal of making his characters universally recognizable is evident in the following anecdote: When Miller directed the play in China in 1983, the

actor playing Happy said, "One thing about the play that is very Chinese is the way Willy tries to make his sons successful. The Chinese father always wants his sons to be dragons."

Willy measures the success of his heroic narrative in the piling up of consumer products. The brand names sprinkled throughout the play – Chevy, Studebaker, Parker House, General Electric, and Hastings ("Whoever heard of a Hastings refrigerator?") are talismans of success in the culture. When Willy visits his boss, Howard, to ask for a raise, it is fitting that Howard is entirely absorbed in his new tech toy, a wire recorder. Howard's success, everything that Willy aspires to, is wrapped up in that device. We can easily imagine the same scene occurring today, swapping out the wire recorder for a smartphone.

A bit later in the scene Willy tells Howard how and when he found his calling as a salesman. He starts by talking about the streak of adventure that ran in the family, how his father had lived for a time in Alaska and how he was on the verge of setting off with his brother Ben to find him, when he was taken with the image of an old salesman, Dave Singleman, who, at the age of eighty four, was still making his living, simply by picking up the phone in his hotel room at the Parker House in Boston, and calling the buyers. It seems to Willy that this is "the greatest career a man could want." He then describes how old Dave died "the death of the salesman" with the hundreds of salesmen and buyers in attendance at the funeral.

It is the story of the birth of Willy's heroic narrative. He may have had other options; we know that his older brother Ben followed their father's more adventurous path, but Willy chooses one that he sees as safer and more stable. As the play unfolds we might well ask, "How's that working for you?" Clearly not well. There may have been a time when Willy was at the top of his sales game, but those days are long past.

The vocation Willy has chosen (or rather that Miller has chosen for him) is doubly significant because it is a profession that accrues very little in the way of a legacy beyond death. Unlike the artist or artisan whose works outlive their maker, the salesman's legacy is limited to the money and possessions accumulated over a lifetime. If that salesman is a failure like Willy, there is no real legacy, no symbolic immortality. Sprinkled throughout the play are clues that Willy senses the emptiness, the insufficiency, of his chosen profession. We hear it in the longing for the trip North not taken. We hear it in his nostalgia for the household fix-up projects at which Willy seems to have some mastery and is able to one-up Charlie. In an exchange between the two, Charlie expresses admiration for the ceiling Willy has managed to put up. Willy responds by insulting Charlie, saying that "A man who can't handle tools is not a man."

In this exchange we hear in Willy "...a screaming for glory as uncritical and reflexive as the howling of a dog...." So deep is his sense of wounded dignity that he is unable to stop himself from lashing out at Charlie, his one true friend. At Willy's funeral, Biff remembers the satisfaction Willy seemed to derive from constructing the front stoop of the house, building the garage and an extra bathroom. Working with one's hands is a motif repeated throughout the play. It suggests that to Willie, Biff, and perhaps Miller, physical labor represents a more authentic identity than one lived solely in the pursuit of money and possessions.

Willy's causa sui project comes up empty, and not just in the final chapters of his life. We may infer that Willy seeks out the Boston Woman (and who knows how many others) to fill the void, and that episode occurs a full 15 years before the few days that make up the "present-day" events of the play. The action Willy takes by sleeping with the Boston Woman plays out literally as karma, Sanskrit for action.

Both Happy and Biff have inherited/been indoctrinated with Willy's heroic narrative. He has raised them to believe, as he does, in this specific shape of the good life. The virtues preached by Willy are personal attractiveness, ambition, and opportunism – what we've come to recognize as values of the American Dream. Such is Willy's answer to cosmic question #2: What are we supposed to do while we're here? The values of this dream apparently do not include studiousness or even much of an ethical core. Biff and Happy seem to have something of a problem respecting the property of others: lumber, basketballs, pens. Perhaps more importantly, Willy repudiates Sartre's great action lesson when he says, "…the sky's the limit because it's not what you do, Ben, it's who you know and the smile on your face! It's contacts, Ben, Contacts!"

In scenes that flash back to the time around Biff's senior year in high school it seems that the matching causa sui projects embraced by Willy and Biff are coming off the rails at the same time. Biff is a promising athlete with the possibility of college ahead of him. "Without a penny to his name, three great universities are begging for him," but he is failing math, and that threatens to prevent him from graduating. His salvation, at least in his imagining, lies in Willy's interceding on his behalf. He travels to Boston to deliver the urgent news, barging in on Willy in his hotel room. Hearing the knocking on the door, Willy hides in the bathroom the buyer he has been "entertaining." A distraught Biff explains to his father how he has flunked math and needs Willy to intercede with the teacher who refuses to grant him the few needed credits. The two share a moment of hilarity as Biff recounts mocking the lisping teacher for the benefit of his classmates – surely the kind of behavior Willy would have encouraged as it props up Biff's likeability with his peers – but just then, hearing the laughter, the Boston Woman bursts in and disrupts the moment.

This is called (in traditional script-analysis jargon) the inciting incident. It is also the reason I have always considered *Death of a Salesman* to be Biff's play, not Willy's. Willy's causa sui project, though failed, is set and certain. The last days of his life chronicled in the play are on a trajectory put in place long ago: the choice of profession, the actions he took along the way – karma – have led inexorably to this moment. There is no arc to Willy's character. The best he can hope for in this final chapter is to tie up some loose ends and make peace with those he loves.

Biff is another story.

Biff's utter adoration of Willy is clear in the above scene. His own heroic narrative is predicated on the rightness of Willy, "the kind of man" he is. In existential terms, Willy embodies the cultural values that shield Biff from all manner of inconvenient vulnerabilities and provide the basis for his own sense of himself as heroic. When Willy is revealed to be a fraud, the foundation on which Biff's identity is constructed cracks wide open. Interestingly, Miller chooses not to show us what happens in the aftermath of Biff's visit to Boston. Miller may have decided that the ferocity of that explosion – a true moment of surrender for Biff – might have been too much to actually portray onstage. Instead, Rashomon-like, Bernard tells the story; how he knew Biff was failing math but felt sure that a solution would emerge from the Boston trip, that Biff was even prepared to go to summer school. But Biff returns defeated. He takes his prized sneakers – the ones he had inscribed with "University of Viginia" – and incinerates them in the furnace. Then he and Bernard have a fistfight during which Bernard is given to understand that Biff has "given up his life." This event marks the end of one heroic narrative and the start of Biff's search for a new one. It doesn't go particularly well.

In the scene, early in the play, where Biff and Happy are camped out in their upstairs bedroom, Biff spins a complex narrative describing a succession of bad jobs in "business of one kind or another," that demand competing with others in a kind of dog-eat-dog manner, while yearning to be in the open air. Yet when he describes being inspired by the beauty of the farm he's working on, he's left with the feeling that he's not getting anywhere, "...wasting my life."

In this speech we recognize that other bit of DNA Biff inherited from Willy, the part about working with his hands and being "outdoors, with your shirt off." Biff has not yet found success, but he's onto the scent of a kind of life that might make him happy. He has come home to give Willy's way one more try, but by the end of the play he will come to the realization, once and for all, that it will never satisfy him. At the funeral, in a last exchange with Happy, we see his determination to stay on the hunt for a more authentic causa sui project. We can also see that Happy is stuck. They get into an argument, graveside, with Biff insisting that Willy had "the wrong dreams" and urging Happy to join him out west. But Happy is not moving. He's going to stick with the Willy dream and succeed.

Willy Loman is one of the iconic roles of the American theater. In a way, he is our Lear. His is the "title role" and he is very much at the center of the play. But for reasons I've already explained, I believe that Biff is the true protagonist of the play. Most theater companies or commercial revivals would not choose to produce *Salesman* without a Willy already in place, and casting builds outward from there. In my view this has served to distort and even undermine the play. Starting with the original Broadway production starring Lee J. Cobb, we tend to remember the major revivals by the names of their Willys: George C. Scott, Dustin Hoffman, Brian Dennehy, Philip Seymour Hoffman. In only one of these do we remember the actor who played Biff, John Malkovich, who appeared opposite

Dustin Hoffman in 1984. Here, finally, was a Biff strong enough to hold the center of the play.

Twelve

Ibsen's Heroic Women: Hedda & Nora

The culture that gives rise to Henrik Ibsen's heroines is beyond oppressive. Rules and regulations are enforced in every arena: money, status, dress, morality, religion, and sexuality. In Ibsen's world, men are men and do manly things; women are women and do womanish things; children are children and do what they're told. Ibsen's own childhood was suffused with wealth and privilege and the expectation that this was a permanent condition. It was not. The family fortune evaporated in bankruptcy, the family relocated and downsized, the father imploded in bitterness and alcoholism. His mother's narrative of suffering is woven into many of his female characters.

A Doll's House

Plays in written form are only blueprints – formal cause – of the product that must come into existence through generous application of moving causes: sets, props, lights, technicians,

Mabou Mines

money, actors. It is sometimes useful, then, to reference specific fully realized productions when we talk about a play. The 2009 Mabou Mines production, adapted and directed by

Lee Breuer, makes a stunning exemplar for the existential framework.

The Mabou Mines production pushes shape to the limit. The men are played by dwarves, the women, especially when in the presence of the men, speak in squeaky little girl voices and walk on their knees so as not to physically dominate the men. The set is composed of fold-out walls – a literal, if somewhat outsized, doll's house. Ringing the stage (at least in the filmed version) are tiers of opera box seats inhabited by marionettes depicting "society" types in white tie, pearls, and gowns. As they look down on the action, reacting "appropriately" (amusement, shock, horror), they are the physical embodiment of the culture that surrounds the world of the play.

The plot of *A Doll's House* charts the parallel, merged heroic narratives of Nora and her husband, Torvald. From the beginning of the play we see how invested she is in his narrative and how hard she works, schemes, and sacrifices to shore it up. The inciting incident of the play occurs years earlier when Nora forges her dead father's signature to secure a loan. She does this to underwrite the family finances which are suffering because of an illness borne by Torvald. In the ensuing years she has paid the loan back in secret, scrimping and saving her household allowance, all the while enduring jabs from Torvald about what a little spendthrift she is.

The play begins with a visit from Nora's old school friend, Mrs. Linde, who hopes to leverage their friendship into employment. Ibsen uses the occasion of the visit to reveal the backstory of Nora's deceit. We also learn that there is a past relationship between Mrs. Linde and an employee of Torvald's at the bank, Nils Krogstad, who happens to be the agent servicing the loan and therefore the custodian of Nora's secret.

In the Mabou Mines production the performance style was pushed to an almost absurd extreme: The little men parade pompously, chests puffed out, making strident pronouncements; the women simper and shuffle obsequiously. The power relationships are thus rendered explicit, everything is on the surface. But as armor thickens it becomes brittle, and as the action moves forward a palpable tension arises; we feel the artifice groaning, the armor cracking under the pressure exerted by the tensions in the story.

The shattering of a heroic narrative that is the fulcrum for so many dramas can come at any point in the story. In *Death of a Salesman* it occurs many years before the first scene in the play when Willy is revealed as a fraud to Biff in the Boston hotel. For Nora it comes near the end of the play when Torvald shows himself to be unworthy of her love and loyalty.

A Doll's House is often viewed as an early expression of feminism, and that is a reasonable interpretation. Indeed, the play was scandalous in its day, and a change in the ending (in which Nora does not leave but instead is seen going in to be with her children) was forced on Ibsen for the German premiere. How unsatisfying it is, though, for the actor who must represent a position – on either side – in a political morality play. Consider the plight of the actor playing Nora, who must carry the banner for all aggrieved womanhood, or the actor playing Torvald, who must stand in for oppressive husbands everywhere. No, something deeper must be found if the portrayal is to be more than two dimensional. That deeper action is personal, not political.

Imagine Torvald as a little boy. From the time he is small he is bombarded with instructions on what it is to be a man in his culture; a successful man, a privileged man. He also learns what it means to be a woman, a wife, and mother from his mother and from observing the way his father treats her. The design of the doll's house he will construct for Nora is well known to him long before he will be required to build one of his own. He will learn the value of money, and there will be nothing more important than the things it can buy. There will be no hesitation in Torvald's construction of his heroic narrative, no uncertainty about the outlines of that identity. In that structure all approval, all validation comes from the outside, from society. There is no true love in that equation – home, wife, children – all are accessories to the causa sui project that carries the label, the successful banker. When it is revealed that Nora has committed a crime, Torvald comprehends instantly that his narrative is about to come crashing down around him. Everything that he is, owns, and has worked his entire life to build, has been endangered by the actions of this woman, never mind that she did it in support of that very narrative.

Nora, too, has grown up with a clear understanding of who she is and who she is to become. She will marry well and have children, and her husband and her home will be the physical manifestations of her success as a woman and a person. Her own success will be entirely contingent on the success of her husband, so when Torvald's illness creates economic uncertainty she rushes in to solve that problem. Doing so openly is out of the question, since she understands intuitively that Torvald must believe he is the central pillar of his family's strength. To be beholden to Nora, whom he enjoys thinking of as a "little squirrel," would be too diminishing. Nora understands how important it is to Torvald to maintain the illusion of his causa sui project. This merging of her own causa sui with his is what she would call "love."

A collision is therefore inevitable as these two runaway trains of identity hurtle towards each other. Of course Torvald is completely unaware that there is an impending crisis, but Nora sees it coming miles away and fights desperately to prevent it from happening. For Torvald the firing of Krogstad, a sub-par employee, is a simple HR decision. Torvald has no idea that Krogstad is in possession of a secret with which he can blackmail Nora. Nora desperately lobbies both Mrs. Linde and Krogstad as the deadly bean-spilling letter is written, deposited in the letter box, not read (breathless suspense), finally opened and read by Torvald. The stakes are life and death; the reading of the letter will trigger the destruction of one or more of the heroic narratives with which we have become so intimately acquainted.

How marvelous that Ibsen, anticipating the experiments of social psychologists by 100 years, has given us the figure of Dr. Rank, who is dying of syphilis. This striking reminder of mortality subtly ups the ante both for the characters in the play and for the audience. As in Sheldon Solomon's experiments, which showed how reminders of our mortality make us cling more fiercely to our worldviews, we find ourselves even more invested in the life-and-death struggle before us.

The letter is read. Torvald explodes and implodes. As his armor crumbles, the true man is revealed – petty, mean-spirited, caring only for the opinions of others, lashing out at Nora for her misdeeds, attacking her for her lack of morals. It is a moment of ugly surrender. But wait, all is not lost! Another letter arrives from Krogstad. Nora's lobbying of Linde and Krogstad seems to have paid off. Krogstad has had a change of heart, the loan is forgiven, the crisis is over. Torvald is ecstatic. The armor can go back on and stay there. He forgives Nora.

For Nora, though, it is too late. In the moment of Torvald's explosion/implosion Nora sees him clearly for the first time. He is a stranger to her now. Is this really the man for whom she sacrificed so much, for whom she schemed and lied, for whom she risked everything to shore up his fortunes and his dignity, for whom she opened her legs, first to allow him to have her sexually and then to bear his children? She is horrified.

If Torvald's heroic narrative is a lie, then so too is Nora's. As his armor crumbles, so does hers. Now she is nothing, shapeless. In the Mabou Mines production, Nora's surrender is made tangible as she strips down to nothing. The blond tresses that have tumbled down her back are revealed to be a wig. Her head is shaved. She is hairless and completely naked. Suddenly she seems to find her true voice, which emerges deep and full. There is nothing for her now but to set off in search of some truer heroic narrative. She cannot, like Torvald, simply put the armor back on and pretend that all is well. For Nora this is not a political statement. This is not a feminist statement. This is existential. But of course politics is existential.

When we fight for human rights – women's rights, gay rights, the rights of people of color – we are fighting for the right of those individuals to construct and defend heroic narratives that contain dignity and authenticity. This is why John Lewis risked death under the batons of thugs while crossing a bridge in Mississippi, or how Nelson Mandela was able to sustain 27 years in prison. In the end the desire for real, authentic, symbolic life seems to trump the fear of actual death. Nora heads out from the wings of her old, sheltered, and pampered but false life onto the stage of her new, hopefully truer existence – absolutely naked.

Until this moment in the play the closest we and Torvald have come to seeing Nora naked – not just physically naked but bare in her desire – is when she dances the Tarantella. Ibsen lived in a kind of self-imposed exile outside of Norway for many years, some of it in Italy. It was there that he encountered the Tarantella, a folk dance that takes its name from the tarantula spider. Legend has it that when bitten the victim must dance – as wildly as possible – to sweat the poison from the body. The "poison" that needs sweating, in this case, is Nora's suppressed sexuality. Torvald enjoys watching and she enjoys performing on this occasion for surrender. The dance allows Nora to temporarily drop the buffering armor of polite society and allow Torvald to see her "naked." She becomes "strange" to him in these moments, firing up his imagination and his libido: "…then I imagine that you are my young bride and that we have just come from the wedding, and I am bringing you for the first time into our home--to be alone with you for the first time--quite alone with my shy little darling!"

Hedda Gabler

Hedda Gabler was supposed to be a star, and everyone knew it. She is the beautiful daughter of the late General Gabler and could have had any man she wanted. She chose Tesman because he seemed to have a promising future as an academic and was the best prospect on offer at the time. During the

Brenda Withers as Hedda

honeymoon abroad, Tesman, whose area of expertise is "domestic crafts in the Middle Ages," seems to have spent much of the time doing research. Hedda has come to realize that he is an insufferable pedant – a boring, boring man.

Hedda's old schoolmate, Mrs. Elvsted, visits, and we learn that Eilert Løvborg, Hedda's former flame (and rival of Tesman) is back in town. Mrs. Elvsted has been in a loveless marriage with a man 20 years her senior. Løvborg was the tutor to his children, her stepchildren. The relationship between Løvborg and Mrs. Elvsted was thus kindled. With the help of her spiritual guidance, while also serving as his writing muse, he seems to have successfully battled back alcoholism. The ostensible purpose of her visit is to enlist Hedda in her campaign to keep Løvborg from falling off the wagon, a danger now that he is back in town. Another probable motive is to let Hedda know of their involvement and warn her off. It seems Mrs. Elvsted has abandoned her husband and children, a rather reckless act for that era. We might even think of Mrs. Elvsted's narrative as a continuation of Nora's. (*A Doll's House* was written 10 years before *Hedda*.)

The six-month honeymoon and the new house were rather extravagant expenses undertaken by Tesman with the expectation that he would soon secure a position at the University. In fact, Tesman seems to have only the most tentative grasp of the fiscal hole he is digging for himself. Most of the financial transactions have been arranged by Judge Brack, a family friend. It is Brack who delivers the news that Løvborg has published a book that has become something of a sensation. Suddenly Løvborg is a possible competitor for the position seemingly promised to Tesman. Brack's visit with Hedda early in the play makes clear that he hopes to turn her dissatisfaction with Tesman to his own sexual advantage. She declines.

Hedda's real problem – her fatal flaw – is that, on one hand, she's grown up believing that great things are in store for her. She has the beauty and the breeding that should add up to a great heroic narrative. But Hedda has no purpose in life. Like the adolescent who fancies herself some kind of star but has no visible talent for anything, she has been unable to arrive at a suitable causa sui project. Judge Brack suggests that the solution might be found in motherhood, but Hedda rejects this out of hand:

> *HEDDA: Quiet. You'll never see anything like that.*
> *BRACK: We'll talk about it again in a year's time, at the very latest.*
> *HEDDA: I don't have any talent for that, Judge. I don't want anything to do with that kind of calling.*
> *BRACK: Why shouldn't you, like most other women, have an innate talent for a vocation that –*
> *HEDDA: Oh, please be quiet. I often think I only have one talent, one talent in the world.*
> *BRACK: And what is that may I ask?*
> *HEDDA: Boring the life right out of me. Now you know.*

Once Ibsen has arranged the chess pieces, he brings Løvborg onto the board. In his first encounter with Hedda we learn that he has produced a new work in collaboration with his muse, Mrs. Elvsted. The book is his cris de coeur, his masterpiece. It is a sequel to his current book, the one making a splash, which he dismisses as having "not much to it."

> *BRACK: But everyone's been praising it so highly.*
> *LØVBORG: Exactly as I intended-so I wrote the sort of book that everyone can agree with.*

Løvborg explains that the new book is about "the future."

> *TESMAN: The future. Good Lord! We don't know anything about that.*
> *LØVBORG: No, we don't – but there are still one or two things to say about it, just the same. (Opens the package.) Here, you'll see.*

TESMAN: That's not your handwriting is it?
LØVBORG: I dictated it. It's written in two sections.
   The first is about the cultural forces which will
   shape the future and this other section. is about
   the future course of civilization.
TESMAN: Extraordinary. It would never occur to
   me to write about something like that.
HEDDA: Hmm, no, no.

Ibsen has created, in Hedda, a character who is essentially a black hole; a super nova with an insatiable negative core poised to suck everything inside that might come into its orbit. The protagonist in a drama often has the most vital heroic narrative, which then founders on the rocks of some trauma and must be rebuilt. We care about that journey because, in a different shape, it is our journey. Biff is the big man on campus until he has a rude awakening in a Boston hotel room. Nora is a wife and mother, married to a good man, until she learns it's all a sham.

Hedda has nothing but her looks and her family name, but she is surrounded by secondary characters who somehow seem to be pursuing vital causa sui projects. Tesman, for all his bland ineptitude, strives to be an academic star (never mind that no one else is likely to get very excited about his project.) Judge Brack is, well, a judge – the very pillar of society – and seems to draw his sense of heroism from his ability to assert power over others.

Løvborg, though an academic like Tesman, is more truly an artist, for his heroism is earned in the creation of a work of art, his futuristic "sequel." The passage from Becker I quoted earlier would seem to perfectly describe Løvborg the man-god. Even Hedda repeatedly visualizes him with "vine-leaves in his hair," a reference to the god Dionysus:

> *What right do you have to play God? Es-*
> *pecially if your work is great, absolutely*
> *new and different. You wonder where to get*
> *authority for introducing new meanings into*

*the world, the strength to bear it. Your very
work accuses you; it makes you feel inferior.*

Becker's insight helps us understand the torment that seems
to suffuse Løvborg's whole being. He drinks, he sets himself up
for a fall by agreeing to attend Brack's stag party, in the course
of which he loses the manuscript of his great new work. The
manuscript is recovered by Tesman, who delivers it into Hedda's
hands. This will end badly, since, in the absence of a compelling
heroic narrative for herself, she can only derive satisfaction from
destroying the narratives of everyone around her. Tesman, Brack,
Elvsted, Løvborg – all are destroyed by her negative actions.

If Hedda Gabler had been born male she would have
inherited a much broader range of shapes within which
to realize her heroic ambitions. The son would become a
husband, a father, perhaps a leader. All Hedda could inherit
was ambition, a sense of entitlement, and nothing to pour
that heroic narrative into but marriage and motherhood. But
as she tells Brack, "Be quiet! Nothing of that sort will ever
happen!" In the end she destroys herself with the pistol that
is the symbol of her father's power, the causa sui project that
should have been hers to inherit but that she was denied,
perhaps because she was a woman. In her stunning display
of negative actions, Hedda becomes a great antihero.

THIRTEEN

CHEKHOV'S PEOPLE: A SEARCH FOR MEANING

If there is a refrain heard throughout the plays of Anton Chekhov it is a call for meaning. Each character cries out for a sense of purpose, for something to do. It is as if each one is striving toward an answer to our cosmic question #2: What are we supposed to do while we're here?

For Ivanov, the essential question – what to do – is superseded by the even more essential question of whether, in the absence of meaning, it is possible to be at all. He joins the two questions explicitly in this literal invocation of Hamlet when he says:

> what I cannot bear is my own self-loathing. I
> shall die with shame from the thought that I, a
> strong, healthy man, have become a Hamlet,
> a Manfred, one of those "alienated" men...
> or God only knows what!

At the start of the play we find him in this condition:

> To look upon me must be horrifying; and I
> myself don't understand what will become of
> my soul...

And yet he seems willing to at least flirt with the possibility that love or sex may offer some respite. Every night he escapes his home and stultifying marriage to Anna Petrovna to spend time with the beautiful Sasha, 15 years his junior. These transactions with Sasha offer moments of surrender:

> *She speaks to me of love, me, an old man, almost, and I'm intoxicated, I forget about everything else on earth, I'm hypnotized by it, as if by music, and I cry: "A new life! happiness!"*

But even this euphoria is fleeting:

> *And yet the very next day I believe in this life and this happiness as much as I believe in ghosts...*

While the plot contrives to deliver a happy ending to Ivanov – Anna Petrovna dies and a marriage to Sasha is imminent – Ivanov's despair, his emptiness (like Anna's condition) is incurable. In the end he shoots himself.

Death – by suicide, by duel, by disease, by the axe – continually hovers in the background of all Chekhov's plays, providing that essential reminder of mortality to the audience as surely as Sheldon Solomon's researchers demanding that test subjects write short essays imaging the moment of their death. On the very first page of *Ivanov* we are given this exchange with Borkin, his estate steward:

> *BORKIN: You won't believe it, my friend, but we covered over ten miles in three hours...I'm all worn out...My heart, feel how it's beating...*
> *IVANOV:* (Reading.) *Good, I will, later.*
> *BORKIN: No, feel it, now.* (Takes IVANOV's hand and puts it on his chest.) *Do you hear it? Ta-ta-ta-ta-ta-ta. Sounds like I've got heart trouble. Any minute and I might die a sudden death. Listen, will you be sorry if I drop dead?*

IVANOV: I'm reading...later...
BORKIN: No, seriously, will you be sorry if I drop
    dead? Nikolai Alekseevich, will you or won't you
    be sorry if I die all of a sudden?

In *The Seagull* we find each character, even the secondary ones, defining a heroic narrative in relation to the notion of art and artist. Even Shamrayev, who runs the day-to-day affairs of the estate and bullies everyone by controlling who will and won't get use of the horses, fancies himself a theater aficionado. Each time he appears he is in the midst of dominating the conversation by demonstrating his depth of knowledge:

SHAMRAYEV: (entering with Arkadina and the others) *At the Poltava Festival in '73 she gave an amazing performance! Pure delight! A marvelous performance! And whatever happened to the comedian Chadin, Pavel Semyonich Chadin? His Rasplyuyev was immortal, better even than Sadovsky's, I swear to you, my esteemed lady. Where is he now?*

The central characters each occupy a specific perch in the professional world. Arkadina is the established star, but we come to understand that her style of acting and the world in which she moves is precisely the sort of calcified conventional theater her son Treplev finds so appalling and hopes to reinvent. Even as he makes no secret of his disdain we see that Treplev is envious of his mother's success and money, if for no other reason than that he understands how someone like Nina is turned off by his poverty and lack of success. Arkadina's lover, the writer Trigorin, is not quite a star but a true journeyman. He writes continually and enjoys the fame and money that come with his success. He is also acutely aware of his second-rate status. Discussing his fame with Nina he says:

> *Meanwhile, the public is reading: "Yes, it's*
> *charming, it's witty, but Tolstoy it's not," or*
> *"Wonderful, but Turgenev's Fathers and Sons*
> *is better." And so, to my dying day, it will*
> *always be "charming and witty," "charming*
> *and witty" — and never anything more, and*
> *when I'm dead and gone, all my friends will*
> *say, as they file past my grave: "Here lies*
> *Trigorin. He was a good writer, but not as*
> *good as Turgenev."*

Notice that he frames these remarks in relation to "my grave." Paraphrasing psychologist Otto Rank, Ernest Becker describes how the artist uses art to find a solution to the "problem" of existence:

> *...but when you no longer accept the collec-*
> *tive solution to the problem of existence, then*
> *you must fashion your own. The work of art*
> *is, then, the ideal answer of the creative type*
> *to the problem of existence as he takes it in.*

When we look at each of *The Seagull's* artists in the light of Becker's definition, we begin to understand the insecurities of the star Arkadina, whose sense of herself as heroic is more caught up in her own fading physical beauty and accumulation of money than in the actual work of the theater. Trigorin seems more the true artist, always trying to capture something elusive in his writing, usually failing, but always trying. Treplev too is tortured by his lack of ability, especially in comparison to the craftsman Trigorin, who:

> *...has technique, it's easy for him...He's got a*
> *"broken bottle neck gleaming on the bank,"*
> *a "mill wheel casting a somber shadow" —*
> *and presto — there's his moonlit night right*
> *there. And what do I have — "the shimmering*

> *light," and "the soft twinkling of the stars,"*
> *and "the distant sounds of the piano reced-*
> *ing into the quiet, fragrant air"...I mean, it's*
> *unbearable!*

The failure of the art object pushes each of them to fill the persistent void with love, sex, and connection with others. Treplev reaches desperately for Nina and for the love and approval of his mother. Arkadina is simultaneously drawn toward and repulsed by her son, who mostly reminds her of her own aging and mortality. It doesn't help that he continually condemns what he perceives to

Adam Klem as Treplev in
The Seagull at WHAT

be her hackneyed art. Trigorin's emptiness can be only temporarily sated by the youth and infatuation of a Nina. (We wonder how many other Ninas he may have burned through.)

Nina is drawn romantically toward Trigorin, but we sense that her need for him has as much or more to do with her journey toward defining herself as "an artist." She is infatuated as much with the idea of the artist she might learn to become by being with him as she is with him as a man. ("...in return I would demand fame, real fame!") Later, when she has begun to make a career, we hear both from Treplev and from Nina herself just how awful she was on stage:

> *I became — I don't know — mediocre, pitiful,*
> *my acting made no sense any more...I didn't*
> *know what to do with my hands, how to stand*
> *on stage, how to control my own voice. You*
> *have no idea how it feels, to know you're acting*
> *badly.*

Returning to Rank and Becker, Nina has experienced the awful fact that once the work exists the artist is:

stuck with the work of art itself. Like any material achievement it is visible, earthly, impermanent. No matter how great it is, it still pales in some ways next to the transcending majesty of nature; and so it is ambiguous, hardly a solid immortality symbol. In his greatest genius man is still mocked.

But Nina is somehow able to push past what must be a near-paralyzing feeling of inadequacy. She describes a new sense of surrender in the act of performing:

No, I'm not like that any more...I'm a true actress now, and I perform with joy, with ecstasy, I'm intoxicated on the stage, and I feel beautiful.

In the end, *The Seagull* is Nina's play. Of all the artists assembled she suffers the most in her life and in her art and yet comes through with her soul intact. She has thrown herself at Trigorin and been rejected but doesn't dwell on that loss. Her journey has mainly been about finding the equilibrium between her life and her art, and we sense that she has begun to find it. She could stay with Treplev, who would shower her with adoration, but this is not what she wants or needs. By contrast, when Nina walks out of Treplev's life, he is left with nothing. His art alone is not enough to sustain him and so he kills himself.

A motif that runs through many of Chekhov's plays is the transactional investment by those deemed ordinary in those who are perceived to be gifted in some way. We see this in most of the secondary characters of *The Seagull*: Masha, Shamrayev, Sorin, Dorn, and Paulina. In Uncle Vanya the motif surfaces again when Vanya realizes how all of them have been taken in by Serabryakov, the scholar and husband of his late sister:

> *Of course, I'm jealous! And what success with*
> *women! Don Juan himself never knew such*
> *success! His first wife, my sister, a lovely, gentle*
> *creature, pure as that blue sky up above, noble,*
> *warm-hearted, with far more admirers than he*
> *ever had students, — loved him as only the purest*
> *of angels above can love others as pure and per-*
> *fect as themselves. My mother, his mother-in-law,*
> *worships him till this day, till this very day he*
> *inspires in her a kind of religious awe. His sec-*
> *ond wife, a beauty, a fine woman — you just saw*
> *her, — married him when he was already an old*
> *man, gave up her youth for him, her beauty, her*
> *freedom, her radiance. What for? Why? Tell me.*

The investment has revealed itself to be a cruel hoax. Serabryakov turns out to be a talentless nonentity, a complete fraud. At the root of Vanya's bitterness is the realization that in carrying water for the professor he has squandered any possibility of developing a heroic narrative of his own:

> *I worshipped him and his scholarship, I lived and*
> *breathed for him! Every word he wrote, every phrase*
> *he uttered, to me was a stroke of genius…My God, and*
> *now? Now he's retired, and now we see the sum total*
> *of his life: not one single page of his work will live*
> *after him, he's a complete unknown, he doesn't exist! A*
> *soap bubble! And I am betrayed…I see it — foolishly*
> *betrayed…*

Astrov would appear to be a character firmly in charge of his heroic narrative. He is that quintessentially "useful" character of Chekhov's, the doctor. Yet the doctor is disillusioned, burned out. What-

Stacy Fischer and Jeff Zinn in *Uncle Vanya* at Harbor Stage Company

195

ever calling or passion for his vocation he might have had appears to have been snuffed out by the unstoppable progression of misery and ignorance that presents itself to him day in and day out:

> *Third week of Lent, I went to Malitskoe for the epidemic... Typhus... they bring the switch-man over from the railroad yard; I lay him out on the table, you know, for surgery, and he up and dies on me under chloroform. Just like that. Right on the spot. And that's when my feelings come alive again, just when I don't need them...and my conscience starts to torment me, as if I'd killed him myself, on purpose...*

In the absence of a purposeful causa sui Chekhov's characters fill the void in the ways humans always seek to fill the void: love, sex (or sex masquerading as love), drink, drugs, talk, talk, talk. Yelena presents a kind of bright shiny object for both Astrov and Vanya to pursue. Astrov is a drinker, if not a drunk, and also busies himself with the cause of conservation. His knowledge of and passion for this cause make up a large part of his heroic self-narrative. He also uses it as part of his arsenal of seduction. Vanya, in his despair, steals morphine from Astrov in a drive toward oblivion and possible self-annihilation.

The women in the play struggle no less with their lack of meaning and purpose. A character as tertiary as the old nurse Marina seems to find meaning in the simple task of knitting. She may be the character most at peace in the play. Her focus is on things outside and larger than herself. She cares for others and invokes a higher power.

Yelena has no heroic narrative of her own. At a very young age she placed a bet by marrying the professor, thinking, like all the others, that he was bound for glory. Several mentions of her piano playing offer hints of an unfulfilled talent, but near the end of Act II the suggestion  ately shut down by Serabryakov, who is trying to sleep. The language she uses to describe herself to Sonia is as a minor character; inconsequential, tedious, worthless, futile, tiresome, of no importance (depending on the translation).

Justin Campbell and Amie Lytle in *Uncle Vanya* at Harbor Stage Company

When Sonia suggests that she busy herself by helping others, she brushes off the suggestion, recognizing that a choice like that, for her, would be forced and inauthentic. More than anything, she seems to derive satisfaction from the power her beauty exerts over others.

Sonia dreams of a love with Astrov and, like Marina, puts her faith in god. She returns to work and faith when everything else has gone away. In the final scene, Chekhov entrusts her with conveying us out of the play and back into our lives:

> *What can we do, we must live! We shall live,*
> *Uncle Vanya. We shall live through the end-*
> *less, endless row of days, the long evenings,*
> *we shall patiently bear the ordeals that fate*
> *has in store for us; we shall toil for others*
> *now and in our old age, we shall know no*
> *rest, and when our hour comes, we shall die*
> *humbly, and there beyond the grave we shall*
> *say that we've suffered, that we've wept, that*
> *life was bitter, and God will take pity on us,*

The need for work, for a useful vocation, for a meaningful causa sui project that creates meaning beyond itself recurs throughout all of the plays. Work offers a narrative for our journey toward death, or away from it if we are in denial.

Chekhov's characters seem to carry the awareness that they are at the mercy of gigantic forces of culture and history. Time and again we hear them wondering about what the world will be in 100 or 200 years and how their world will appear to that new, more enlightened one. Chekhov's genius was to notice the tectonic plates on which he and all of Russia were standing and that were moving slowly, inexorably toward an uncertain future. As the plates grind and move there is little to do but love, work, and talk. Something meaningful must be done.

Fifty years before Sartre, we find Chekhov telling stories of people who seem unable to act, and pay the price for their inaction. The three sisters, Irina, Masha, and Olga, dream and talk continually about someday going to Moscow. Vershinin too seems mostly to want to talk, although his talk includes the usual paean to "work":

> *It seems to me that everything on earth must change, little by little, indeed, it is changing even now, right before our very eyes. After two hundred – three hundred years, after a thousand years, even, — it's not the length of time that matters — a new life will finally dawn, a life of happiness. And we shall not take part in that life, of course, but we are living for it now, we are working for it, yes, even suffering for it, we are creating it — and this, and this alone, is our reason for being, indeed, this is our happiness.*

In *Three Sisters* the urgency of finding something to do presents itself most forcibly in the character of Irina, who says:

> *A man must work, he must work by the sweat of his brow, whoever he may be, and this and this alone is his reason for being, his happiness, his ecstasy. ...Merciful God, let alone a human being, better to be an ox, better to be a humble horse, even, if only to work, better that than a young lady, who gets up at noon each day, who drinks coffee in bed, who takes*

two hours to get dressed...

In that passage she seems to be describing Yelena in *Uncle Vanya* – the worst possible curse. She is answered by Tuzenbach, who typifies the stratum of the Russian culture Chekhov knew best and chronicled most thoroughly:

> *A longing for work, oh dear God, how well I understand it! I have never worked a day in my life. I was born in Petersburg, cold and idle Petersburg, into a family which never had a care in the world. I remember, when I'd arrive home from military school, a valet would pull off my boots.*

They seem to sense the coming revolution. Tuzenbach again:

> *For the time has come when great thunderclouds are gathering over us, a strong, healthy storm is brewing, drawing nearer and nearer, and soon it shall blow away idleness, indifference, prejudice against work, and putrefying boredom. I shall work, and in twenty-five – thirty years or so, every man shall work. Each and every man!*

Irina returns to the theme a few pages later:

> *You say that life is beautiful. Yes, perhaps it is, but what if only seems to be! For us, for we three sisters, life has not been beautiful, life has choked us, like weeds...I'm weeping. I mustn't weep...(Hastily wipes away the tears, smiles.) Work, we must work. That is why we're so sad, why we look upon life with such*

sorrow, because we are strangers to work.
We are born of those who disdained work...

The brother, Andrey, moves in and out of the action like a ghost. He is another character with no successful *causa sui* project to sustain him. Like Ivanov, Vanya, or even Serabryakov, he is a man who once had potential but whose ambitions and opportunities have evaporated, leaving behind a kind of empty shell. Masha observes:

There's Andrey, our little brother... All hopes lost. Once, thousands of people lifted a great bell, with much toil and travail, a fortune spent to raise it, and then all of a sudden, it fell and shattered. Without warning, without cause. So, too, with Andrey...

Andrey is so isolated he can only open up to Ferapont, who is probably deaf:

Tomorrow is Friday, there won't be a meeting, but I'll go in anyway...I like to keep busy. It's boring at home.... Today, out of sheer boredom, I picked up this book — my old university lectures, and I saw how ludicrous it all was...My God, I am the secretary of the district council, the very council chaired by Protopopov, I am the secretary, and the most I can ever hope for is to become a member of the district council! I who dream every night of becoming a professor at Moscow University, a celebrated scholar, admired throughout all of Russia!

Disappointed in his lack of a meaningful causa sui he has settled for merging with Natasha, even allowing her to push his sisters out of the house.

CHEKHOV'S PEOPLE: A SEARCH FOR MEANING

Eventually Irina's passion for the idea of work bumps up against the reality of what she is actually allowed to do:

> *I must find a new position, this one is not for me. Everything I longed for, everything I dreamed of, and it's nowhere to be found, not there, at least. Work without poetry, without meaning...*

And later in Act III:

> *It's enough, enough! I worked in the telegraph office, now I work for the town council and I hate, no, I despise everything they give me to do...I'm almost twenty-four years old, I've been working forever, and my brain has shrivelled up, I've grown old, and thin, and ugly, and nothing, nothing gives me any satisfaction whatsoever, and meanwhile time passes by, and it's almost as if we're disappearing, fading away from all hope of a truly beautiful life, fading further and further away into some kind of abyss. I despair, and why I'm alive, why I haven't killed myself by now, I don't understand.*

For Irina, exactly like Ivanov, Treplev, or Vanya, suicide seems to be the only way out.

As the play comes to an end the sisters gather together like so many passengers on the deck of the Titanic as it slips under the water. There's even a band providing accompaniment.

In The Cherry Orchard the talk, hopes, and dreams of Madame Ranevskaya and her brother, Gayev, contrast with the action of the merchant Lopakhin. In these contrasting characters we witness the clash of cultural shapes: refined and educated landowners in the process of being pushed aside by workers and merchants. Lopakhin himself is acutely aware of these differences:

> *My papa was a peasant, an ignorant fool, he understood nothing, taught me nothing, he only beat me when he was drunk, and always with a stick. And the fact of the matter is, I'm the same kind of ignorant fool that he was. I never learned anything, I'm ashamed of my own handwriting, it's not even human, it's more like a hoof-mark than a signature.*

Towards the end of the play, after the orchard has been sold – to Lopakhin – and the family is preparing to leave the house, which will be torn down, he has something of a last word:

> *What's going on here? Let there be music! Loud, the way I want it! Let everything be the way I want it! Here comes the new master, the owner of the cherry orchard! (Accidentally shoves against a table, almost turning over a candelabra.) I can pay for it all, for everything!*

For all his supposed coarseness, Lopakhin sees the world and the people in it very clearly. He says this about Gayev, who may land on his feet after all:

> *They say that Leonid Andreich has taken a position at a bank, 6,000 a year...He won't be able to keep it, though, he's too lazy...*

Again and again in Chekhov's plays we see the embodiment of the tenet that a character's primary action is the construction and defense of a project of identity that takes the form of a heroic narrative. And it is not only in his Ivanovs, Vanyas, Treplevs, and Irinas that this quality is present but also in the minor characters. For once we might understand the cliché about there being "no small actors," since each one seems also to be working furiously to assert a sense of meaning and identity. Chekhov's democracy and generosity in this regard add infinite texture to the human landscape of his plays.

There may be no more poignant image than the last entrance of Firs, the ancient servant in *The Cherry Orchard*. After everyone else has gone he suddenly appears, dressed in full livery – reporting for duty, as it were – and, having nothing to do, lies down and dies.

FOURTEEN

HAMLET
GODS AND GHOSTS

In contemporary theater, as in contemporary life, immortal-ity comes mainly in symbolic form. Even in the plays of Ibsen and Chekhov in which religion seems still very much at the center of the culture, characters such as Solness in *The Master Builder* and Trigorin in *The Seagull* prove their heroism through feats of worldly accomplishment – or try to.

Shakespeare's world is quite different. The worldly riches piled up by a Claudius or a Macbeth in the takeover of a kingdom are won at the risk of sealing the gates of heaven and opening the ones to hell. The central premise of this book – that all humans, and therefore all characters, share a core motivation of constructing and defending a heroic narrative – might seem to run aground in a pre-modern world dominated by gods and ghosts. Does the existential framework ap-ply only to plays of the modern era? I think not. We can discern the quest for meaning and a struggle to define identity in characters as ancient as Oedipus and Lysistrata, let alone Hamlet and Juliet. Even in a world with the certain presence of gods and ghosts there is still enough uncer-tainty to fuel existential angst.

Harold Bloom

In *Hamlet: Poem Unlimited*, Harold Bloom writes, "You cannot reduce Hamlet to any consistency, even in his grief,"

Indeed, the conceptual ground covered in Hamlet is vast and Hamlet's own obsessions are many. We find him at various times contemplating heroism/cowardice; madness/sanity; corrupted flesh; the theater: masks/playing/playing badly; mortality/immortality; love; intelligence (wit) and the lack thereof; and word versus action. Yet all of it coheres within the existential framework. Death, and the construction of narrative to elude it, are everywhere in *Hamlet*. Death propels action as it impedes action.

Heroism/Cowardice

Sarah Berhardt as Hamlet

Hamlet's heroic narrative is well established before the inciting events at the start of the play. He is the privileged Prince of Denmark, studying abroad, surrounded by a circle of friends, with a loving mother and father at home and succession to the throne in his future. Then it all goes to hell.

To say that Hamlet's heroic narrative has been shattered is apt, since heroism would definitely be part of a princely job description. He comments on his own lack of courage: "Am I a coward? Who calls me villain? breaks my pate across?... But I am pigeon-liver'd and lack gall....Why, what an ass am I! This is most brave...." It would be too simple, however, to call Hamlet's "problem" a matter of cowardice or even indecision.

Words as Substitute for Action

If, as Kenneth Burke says, language is symbolic action, Hamlet has a real problem with that. Too many of Hamlet's actions are in words, words, words. He considers it his most repulsive character trait. It is the problem he returns to again and again. To be or not to be is not really the question. That throws us off the trail in its explicit invocation of death by suicide as an option. The real question is to act or not to act? He makes this plain in the soliloquy in which he compares himself with the warriors of Fortinbras' army. He begins with the essential question posed by philosophers and sociologists: What sets man apart from other creatures?

> *What is a man,*
> *If his chief good and market of his time*
> *Be but to sleep and feed? a beast, no more.*
> *Sure, he that made us with such large discourse,*
> *Looking before and after, gave us not*
> *That capability and god-like reason*
> *To fust in us unused.*

We are not beasts but rather have sentience and the capacity to look "before and after" at the past and future. To ask, Where do we come from? What are we to do while we're here? Where are we going? So, Hamlet wonders, what's my excuse for not taking action?

> *Now, whether it be*
> *Bestial oblivion, or some craven scruple*
> *Of thinking too precisely on the event,*
> *A thought which, quarter'd, hath but one part wisdom*
> *And ever three parts coward,*
> *I do not know*
> *Why yet I live to say 'This thing's to do;'*
> *Sith I have cause and will and strength and means*
> *To do 't. Examples gross as earth exhort me:*

Too much thinking renders us incapable of action – this is the argument of the whole speech. Hamlet marvels at the ability of Fortinbras, the "delicate prince," to not think so much but rather to act:

> *Witness this army of such mass and charge*
> *Led by a delicate and tender prince,*
> *Whose spirit with divine ambition puff'd*
> *Makes mouths at the invisible event,*
> *Exposing what is mortal and unsure*
> *To all that fortune, death and danger dare,*
> *Even for an egg-shell. Rightly to be great*
> *Is not to stir without great argument,*
> *But greatly to find quarrel in a straw*
> *When honour's at the stake.*

In Hamlet's universe to be great is to be willing to fight and die "even for an eggshell." Yet Hamlet, with far more motivation (again that actor's word), is unable to act:

> *How stand I then,*
> *That have a father kill'd, a mother stain'd,*
> *Excitements of my reason and my blood,*
> *And let all sleep? while, to my shame, I see*
> *The imminent death of twenty thousand men,*
> *That, for a fantasy and trick of fame,*
> *Go to their graves like beds, fight for a plot*
> *Whereon the numbers cannot try the cause,*
> *Which is not tomb enough and continent*
> *To hide the slain? O, from this time forth,*
> *My thoughts be bloody, or be nothing worth!*

Hamlet's consciousness outstrips the conventions – the shape – of his time. He is too enlightened to be blindly driven by his urge to heroism but instead holds back, questioning. Nietzsche makes much the same point in *The Birth of Tragedy*: "Knowledge kills action, action requires the veil of illusion; it is this lesson which Hamlet teaches...."

We feel he is right to say no to the butchering of thousands of young men "for a fantasy and trick of fame" that would create numbers of dead too many to be buried in the plot of land for which they fought. Hamlet here foretells the brutal, futile battles of the 20th century: World War I, Vietnam, and the Falklands, all pointless "quarrels in a straw." Yet even Hamlet – intelligent, knowing, Hamlet – is trapped. "My thoughts be bloody, or be nothing worth!" The tension between the cultural shape he inherits and his questioning of that shape prevents him from simply killing Claudius.

Concluding to be, or not to be:

> *And thus the native hue of resolution*
> *Is sicklied o'er with the pale cast of thought,*
> *And enterprises of great pith and moment*
> *With this regard their currents turn awry,*
> *And lose the name of action.*

Here again is sense warring with sensibility. Hamlet is conquered by too much sense.

Madness

In the scenes that follow Hamlet's encounter with the Ghost, various characters react to his changed affect. The word "mad" is used freely, and we witness some of this so-called mad behavior ourselves. But Hamlet is less mad than discombobulated – out of joint. His inability to act stems from the fact that his idea of himself has been thrown into confusion. Without a clear sense of self there can be no center from which to act. Those around him, baffled by his behavior, have no vocabulary to describe what they are witnessing other than "mad." Hamlet, ever knowing – watching others watching him even as he watches himself – adopts a strategy of exploiting their confusion. He sees that he can play it to his advantage and, if nothing else, buy time as he contemplates his next move.

There are times in the course of the play when Hamlet surrenders to the feelings that are surging within and acts violently or impulsively or unleashes great volleys of words, some of which are difficult for his listeners to comprehend. This unshackled expression is not madness. That it might be labeled such by the others speaks more to the fact that he is violating the cultural codes that dictate "proper" behavior, but isn't this often what gets people classified as crazy?

Corrupted Flesh

There are so many instances in the play where the motif of death is present, which makes the play ripe for our analysis. Harold Bloom says:

> *Hamlet's consciousness is so enormous that it comprehends the whole question of human mortality: we are in some ways like mortal gods and yet we are mortal and we know that we are going to die. That consciousness of death on Hamlet's part makes him, as George Wilson Knight wrote, '...death's ambassador to us. He conveys to us the embassy of death.'"*

Those things that remind us of our corporality can trigger intense revulsion as they remind us that we are far more mortal than god. D.H. Lawrence, who devoted buckets of ink to his own obsession with the flesh, fixated on this aspect of Hamlet's character. In his travel memoir, *Twilight in Italy*, he presents a dramaturgical analysis based on what is essentially a community-theater production of the play. After taking apart each peasant's performance (punching below his weight) he offers:

D.H. Lawrence

> *I had always felt an aversion from Hamlet:*
> *a creeping, unclean thing he seems, on the*
> *stage... His nasty poking and sniffing at his*
> *mother, his setting traps for the King, his*
> *conceited perversion with Ophelia make him*
> *always intolerable. The character is repul-*
> *sive in its conception, based on self-dislike*
> *and a spirit of disintegration.*

Lawrence's theory is that Shakespeare is locating in his central character the epochal shift away from the autocratic and toward the democratic.

There is, I think, this strain of cold dislike, or self-dislike, through much of the Renaissance art, and through all the later Shakespeare. In Shakespeare it is a kind of corruption in the flesh and a conscious revolt from this. A sense of corruption in the flesh makes Hamlet frenzied, for he will never admit that it is his own flesh.

And even though Gertrude is seemingly ignorant of Claudius's crime, Lawrence (conflating Gertrude with other Shakespearean murderesses) somehow manages to blame the women:

> *Yet Gertrude, like Clytemnestra, is the po-*
> *tential murderer of her husband, as Lady*
> *Macbeth is murderess, as the daughters*
> *of Lear. The women murder the supreme*
> *male, the ideal Self, the King and Father...*
> *Hamlet goes mad in a revulsion of rage*
> *and nausea. Yet the women-murderers only*
> *represent some ultimate judgment in his own*
> *soul. At the bottom of his own soul Hamlet*
> *has decided that the Self in its supremacy,*
> *Father and King, must die. It is a suicidal*
> *decision for his involuntary soul to have*
> *arrived at. Yet it is inevitable. The great*
> *religious, philosophic tide, which has been*

swelling all through the Middle Ages, had
brought him there.

Who knew that Hamlet was carrying such a heavy load? Not just the murder of a father to avenge but "the great religious, philosophic tide..." of history.

If theater holds the mirror up to nature it is mostly Lawrence's own nature that is revealed here. In much of his writing he wrestled with his own issues with women and "corruption in the flesh." But he is on to something essential about Hamlet, who frets about his "too, too, sullied flesh":

Fie on't! ah fie! 'tis an unweeded garden,
That grows to seed; things rank and gross
in nature
Possess it merely.

Lawrence's grand, epoch-shifting theory burdens the actor playing Hamlet too much with the playing of a "position." Better to allow Hamlet to wrestle with more personal demons. He is especially repelled by the corruption he sees in his mother:

Nay, but to live
In the rank sweat of an enseamed bed,
Stew'd in corruption, honeying and making
love
Over the nasty sty,—

It is precisely this corruption, this sense of ourselves as animals, "no more significant than a cockroach," that requires some buffering armor, something that might allow for the possibility of transcendence. But the armor – the mask – also induces revulsion in Hamlet; he is too smart not to recognize the untruth implicit in any such masking. He can bear neither the corruption nor the mask that covers it up. Yet somehow he is drawn to the players.

Masks and Players

In the O, what a rogue soliloquy, we get to the paradox inherent in the notion of the verb to act. Acting – playacting – is pretending, yet there can be no pretending when it comes to truly taking action. Much of Hamlet's guilt lies in this recognition that he is more play actor than life actor. He has just been watching the First Player perform and is astonished at his capacity to get worked up over a fiction:

> *What's Hecuba to him, or he to Hecuba,*
> *That he should weep for her? What would he do,*
> *Had he the motive and the cue for passion*
> *That I have? He would drown the stage with tears*
> *And cleave the general ear with horrid speech*

In the "get thee to a nunnery" speech Hamlet returns to the mask as intolerable cover for corruption: "I have heard of your paintings too, well enough; God has given you one face, and you make yourselves another." Later in the graveyard, "Now get you to my lady's chamber, and tell her, let her paint an inch thick, to this favour [death] she must come; make her laugh at that."

Hamlet is revolted by the duplicitousness of the mask, a point made in his very first exchange with Gertrude:

> *Seems, madam! nay it is; I know not 'seems.'*
> *'Tis not alone my inky cloak, good mother,*
> *Nor customary suits of solemn black,*
> *No, nor the fruitful river in the eye,*
> *Together with all forms, moods, shapes of grief,*
> *That can denote me truly: these indeed seem,*
> *For they are actions that a man might play:*
> *But I have that within which passeth show;*
> *These but the trappings and the suits of woe.*

"Trappings and suits" of psychological armor. Shakespeare has wasted no time (speaking through Hamlet, the consummate actor) in condemning what we would call the indicating of emotion. I can easily imagine the acting class led by Hamlet (channeling Susan Batson) screaming at the quaking students, "CUT THE BULLSHIT!"

Hamlet uses theater as a tool for cutting through the bullshit. The target of the attack is often himself, as in the "O what a rogue" speech, in which he marvels at the actor's ability to manufacture emotion when he himself, with far more motivation, is unable to act. At the end of the day, theater is easy, life is hard.

Love

Harold Bloom questions Hamlet's capacity for love: "Despite his passion in the graveyard, we have every reason to doubt his capacity to love anyone, even Ophelia. He does not want or need love: that is his lonely freedom and it provokes the audience's unreasoning affection for him."

Here's where I depart from Bloom. If anything, Hamlet loves too much:

- His purest, least complicated and most reciprocated love is with Horatio.
- It is Hamlet's love for his stern, absent, yet demanding father that propels much of the action of the play.
- Yorick, the dead jester, probably served as a Hamlet's surrogate father, standing in as playmate and mentor, grantor of affection, "…he hath borne me on his back a thousand times…. Here hung those lips that I have kissed I know not how oft."
- The most tortured love relationships – the most difficult *transactions* – are with the two women, Gertrude and Ophelia.

Every one of these relationships make vivid the struggle between Hamlet's desire to individuate and his need to merge.

Bloom locates the "dramaturgical crisis" of the play in the closet scene with Gertrude. Here Shakespeare weaves together Hamlet's love for his father, his mother's betrayal, death (he kills Polonius), and sweaty sex; questioning the propriety of Gertrude, at her age, to still feel lust. It is where we find some of Hamlet's most surrendered speeches. Yet in the end it is just more words. Even as he concludes his verbal fusillade, his passion sputtering out, he says, "I must to England; you know that?" And shortly thereafter he allows himself to be shipped off. Heroic indeed.

Hamlet's outburst at Ophelia's graveside feels over-blown, even narcissistic, but it may be that he is acting out in grief at the loss of what might have been a true and honest partnership in marriage had the Ghost not intruded to derail Hamlet's heroic journey.

FIFTEEN

THE EXISTENTIAL ACTOR

As grandiose a title as *The Existential Actor* may already be, it is probably too small. These questions, challenges, and paradoxes I have been discussing apply to much more than just the concerns of actors. The true subject of the book is human beings, fictional characters created by human beings, and those whose work it is to bring those fictional characters to life: actors, directors, designers, dramaturgs, producers, and technical artists, all of whom are also human beings.

The foundational principal here is that all humans are driven by common desires. We all want to live and to feel that we are alive. We want the roles we inherit or choose for ourselves to be authentic and have meaning. We hope that our brief time on earth will not be forgotten too quickly. These wants, needs, and wishes are timeless and are universal. They are not modern inventions, nor are they applicable only to those of us who live in the western world. They inhabit the oldest narratives we have. As much as humanity may have learned and grown and changed, there is more commonality than difference between us and our ancestors.

It is this commonality that I have relied on as I forged my synthesis of techniques and traditions of storytelling, character creation, and character interpretation. The term "existential" feels both modern and quaint, perhaps a relic of the '50s when beatniks in turtlenecks first appropriated Sartre. Cool trends may be "born astride of a grave," to borrow from Samuel Beckett, but the essence of existentialism is survival. The urge to survive is as old as life and has no sell-by date.

Everywhere we look, people are pursuing their heroic narratives, small and grand. Each one is somehow declaring their allegiance to a group, and at the same time asserting their very particular individuality. Where I live on Cape Cod, a certain figure is ubiquitous: the bearded man in the beat up pickup truck, work clothes, longish hair. Sometimes the bumper stickers further clarify allegiances: guns, either for or against; Obama, either for or against. The cover does not necessarily define the book. In either case a close look and a conversation reveal a fierce glint of conviction in the eye, a determination to fulfill the particular *causa sui* project under way. There are "stock characters" everywhere, but a second look reveals a deeply individuated, highly complex *person*. It takes a great storyteller to render specificity of character in a fictional creation.

Fictional characters almost always mirror the shape, or some facet of the shape, of their creators. Shakespeare's rare genius was expressed in his ability to create so many – almost 100 – individuated major characters. It may be this astonishing ability of his to transcend his own shape that has given rise to theories that he could not have been the sole creator of the works. The existential lens and the four elements – which are merely a synthesis of the many useful techniques and technical focal points discovered and explored by theater practitioners throughout history – allow us to think about the characters we create or interpret in a way that goes to the source of human motivations.

In rehearsal I don't talk much about the theory that is central to this book. As I watch and listen and do my best to guide actors toward realizing the play we're working on and how they fit into it, I am guided by the ideas myself, but rarely mention death denial, heroic narratives, *causa sui* projects, and the rest of it. There isn't enough time. In the classroom, however, I do talk about it and do what I can to communicate the imperatives of Maslow's pyramid; how survival is the foundation for thinking about what motivates us all.

How might these ideas translate into a specific program for training? I have often felt that the best approach might be to assemble a team of specialists. Modules in *shape, action, transaction,* and *surrender* would gather together instructors whose backgrounds and specific skill sets would allow them to take the student deep into those areas.

The *Shape* department includes instructors trained in Alexander technique for body alignment, Linklater for vocal production, coaches for specific accent and dialect work, perhaps a Delsartian (they exist). There are classes in period dance – so much of how people moved in various periods and cultures was informed by the court and social dancing. Shape exercises demand total physical transformations, with attention to gesture, movement, dialect, costume, and makeup. There are workshops in mask, Viewpoints, and clowning. The Michael Chekhov specialist takes us through the strong forms of *psychological gesture* exercises. Of course each character exists in the context of a specific culture which suggests the need for an in-depth study of the history and socio-political background of the play.

In the *Action* department I look for teachers who are already well versed in the Stanislavskian vocabulary of motivation, intention, objective, and what is sometimes called *actioning. Actions: The Actors' Thesaurus* by Marina Calderone and Maggie Lloyd-Williams, might be a useful text for the action class. Action exercises are similar to those done in acting classes everywhere: text is broken down into units/beats with objectives, intentions, and actions chosen. We make decisions about the spine of the play – it's *dianoia* – and the super-objective of the characters – their overarching goal in the play. The difference here is that actors are asked to consider how the heroic narrative of the character drives all the other actions. An exercise that makes this salient is *talk or die:* An actor stands in the center of a circle. He then makes a case for why he should be allowed to live. Participants in the outer circle listen. If they are moved or convinced by the argument they stay where they are. If they are not convinced, they take a step in towards the talker. When they reach him he dies. Fun!

For the *Transactional* piece we rely on teachers trained in Meisner repetition exercises. If we're lucky, Patsy Rodenburg is on hand to school students in second circle exercises. Students are asked to pay attention to the day-to-day transactions they engage in with peers, strangers, and significant others. We bring in social psychologists to share with us their experiments and current developments in the field of interpersonal dynamics.

To encourage students to *surrender* we enlist any and every technique available that allows us to strip away our psychological armor and express ourselves. This does not mean that we engage in classroom psychoanalysis or subject anyone to the sort of brutal shock tactics that have sometimes been employed by acting teachers. Rather we encourage those who might benefit from therapy to seek it out on their own with a trusted practitioner. Before we are able to fully explore characters who are very different from ourselves, a certain amount of self-reflection and insight is necessary. It is important that the actor have a firm grasp of her own shape and heroic narrative. The actor must take stock of her own cultural influences and become consciously aware of how she already walks, talks, dances, sings, and tells stories. I ask actors to tell the story of themselves and how they imagine others might tell that story about them. The classroom is a safe space where we dance and shout, bellow and cry, and are allowed to behave again like children.

In chapter two I described the actor in the wings as a "desperate hero," because the essence of acting requires leaping bravely into a dangerous void. Each time the actor takes the stage she is stepping into an unknown future. Both the actor and the character carry with them a fundamental motivating action, which is to construct and defend the heroic narrative, however it has been shaped. That shape is not simply an overlay of dialect, costume, posture, gesture, etc. but an entire culture specific to the play and that character, a culture that was responsible for conveying to the actor/character what that heroic narrative should be in the first place. As that actor/character ventures onto the stage and into the world of the play (ideally in second circle) she will encounter others – not just the other characters that populate the stage world, but also the audience – Grotowski's spectators – from whom the actor/character will receive signals of success or failure. That *transaction* will require *achtung* and Meisnerian listening.

As the character carries the action forward, conveying accurately the shape that has been ordained by the culture and listening hard for the signals of success or failure in every transaction, there may come a moment when the narrative is interrupted, when the transaction delivers only failure, and when the character armor – so carefully constructed to buffer the actor/character from the awful chaos just outside the safety zone – is cracked open. Then the actor/character will be forced to surrender to that overpowering reality that has been so carefully kept at bay.

Where does the audience figure in all this? Is there any reason the audience should care about the mechanics behind the performances they witness? The existential struggle taking place on stage is of direct concern to every member of the audience, each of whose own struggle is very much under way. It may be because the spectator is wholly wrapped up in his or her own heroic narrative that the theater is so enduring as an art form. In the theater we bear witness to other human beings, shaped like ourselves or perhaps utterly different, who are grappling with the project of being human, of creating meaning in their lives. As spectators we get to try on those different shapes. We identify with or reject the choices we are offered from the stage. Those choices may affirm or violate our sense of right and wrong, our own sense of order and meaning. By the time we leave the theater we may have some new perspective on who we are and who those other people are that we encounter on the street, in our lives, and in the world.

I have tried to be mindful of my own *causa sui* project and the through-line in my life, asserting my own value and right to exist. Communicating the core ideas of this book has certainly become something of a cause for me, and I strive to be aware of how much I am invested in the success or failure of that project. To quote Becker once more, "The most that any one of us can seem to do is to fashion something–an

221

object or ourselves–and drop it into the confusion, make an offering of it, so to speak, to the life force." This book has been my attempt to do just that.

BIBLIOGRAPHY

Titles are listed under the chapter heading in which they first appear and may be cited again in subsequent chapters.

Introduction

Eugene Ionesco, *The Killer*, Grove Press, 1960

Sheldon Solomon, et al, *Tales From The Crypt: On The Role Of Death In Life*, in *Zygon: Journal of Religion and Science,* vol. 33, no. 1 (March 1998)

Ernest Becker, *The Denial of Death,* Free Press 2007

Chapter 1

Sheldon Solomon, *In the Wake of 9-11: The Psychology of Terror* By Tom Pyszczynski, PhD, Sheldon Solomon, PhD, and Jeff Greenberg, PhD American Psychological Association (APA) 2003

Søren Kierkegaard, *The Concept of Dread* Princeton University Press; 2nd edition, 4/1/68

Annie Hall, film by Woody Allen, 1977

Sheldon Solomon, *Human Awareness of Mortality and the Evolution of Culture* in The Psychological Foundations of Culture, Psychology Press, 2003

Louis CK, *Live At The Beacon Theater,* December 10, 2011

Martin Heidegger, *Introduction to Metaphysics,* Yale University Press, 2014

Phillipe Rochat , *Five Levels Of Self-Awareness As They Unfold Early In Life* in Consciousness and Cognition 12, 2003

Pew Research Center's Religion & Public Life Project: Religious Landscape Survey, 2014

Henry David Thoreau, *Civil Disobedience and Other Essays*

Jean Paul Sartre, *Existentialism is a Humanism*, 1946

Chapter 2

Rodney A. Brooks et al, *Challenge Problems for Artificial Intelligence* in Proceedings of AAAI-96, Thirteenth National Conference on Artificial Intelligence, Portland, Oregon, August 1996

E. O. Wilson, *Consilience: The Unity of Knowledge* Vintage, 1999

Chapter 3

Radio interview with Terry Gross, *Fresh Air* WHYY April 13, 2011

Jay Malarcher, *The Actor as Literary Critic*

Aristotle, *The Poetics*

Aristotle, *Metaphysics*

Jody Enders, *The Farce of the Fart* and Other Ribaldries, University of Pennsylvania Press, 2013

Harold Bloom, *Shakespeare: The Invention of the Human,* Riverhead Trade, 1999

Shakespeare, *Hamlet,* Act II sc ii

Richard Flecknoe in *A Short Discourse of the English Stage* in Laurence Oliver, *On Acting*, Simon & Schuster,1986

John Barrymore "To Be Or Not To Be" on YouTube

Denis Diderot, *The Paradox of Acting*, Kessinger Publishing, 2007

François Joseph Talma, *Talma on the Actor's Art,* Kessinger Publishing, 2010

Michel W. Pharand, *Bernard Shaw and the French,* University Press of Florida, 2001

Elsie M Wilbor, *Delsarte Recitation Book,* Ulan Press, 2011

Chapter 4

Jean Benedetti, *Stanislavski: His Life and Art,* Methuen Drama, 1999

Constantin Stanislavski, *My Life in Art ,* Theatre Arts Book, 1952

Jonathan Pitches, *Science and the Russian Tradition,* Routledge, 2005

Robert Lewis, *Method or Madness,* Samuel French, 1958

Mel Gordon, *The Stanislavski Technique: Russia, A Workbook for Actor*s, Applause Theatre & Cinema Books, 2000

Robert Leach, *Vsevolod Meyerhold (Directors in Perspective)*, Cambridge University Press, 1993

Frederick Taylor, *The Principles of Scientific Management*, Martino Fine Books, 2014

Harold Clurman, *The Fervent Years,* Da Capo Press 1983

Stanislavski, *An Actor Prepares,* Theatre Arts Books, 1963

Sanford Meisner, *On Acting,* Vintage, 2012

David Garfield, *The Actors Studio: A Player's Place,* Macmillan, 1980

Susan Batson, *Truth: Personas, Needs, and Flaws in The Art of Building Actors and Creating Characters,* Rugged Land, 2007

Sanford Meisner, *On Acting,* Vintage, 1987

Kim Durham, *Acting on and off: Sanford Meisner Reconsidered*, Studies in Theatre & Performance, Volume 23, Number 3, December 2004

Edward Dmytryk, *On Screen Acting,* Focal Press, 1984

Sanford Meisner Master Class on DVD

Bruder, Cohn, Olnek, et al, *A Practical Handbook for the Actor,* Vintage, 2012

David Mamet, *True and False: Heresy and Common Sense for the Actor,* Vintage, 2011

Chapter 5

Susan Sontag essay in The New York Review of Books, Feb 1963

Antonin Artaud, *The Theater and Its Double,* Grove Press, 1958

Jerzy Grotowski, *Towards a Poor Theatre,* Odin Teatrets, 1968

Bertolt Brecht, *Brecht on Theatre: The Development of an Aesthetic,* Hill and Wang, 1964

Jennifer Lavy, *Theoretical Foundations of Grotowski's Total Act, Journal of Religion and Theatre,* Vol. 4, No. 2, Fall 2005. 175-188

Arthur Holmberg, *The Theatre of Robert Wilson,* Cambridge University Press, 2005

Arthur C. Holmberg, L.A. Times Article: *The Merlin of the Avant-Garde...* August 08, 1993 http://articles.latimes.com/1993-08-08/magazine/tm-21816_1_robert-wilson/5

Herbert Blau, *To All Appearances: Ideology And Performance,* Routledge, 1992

Mary Overlie website - http://www.sixviewpoints.com/Theory_1.html

Anne Bogart/Tina Landau, *The Viewpoints Book: A Practical Guide to Viewpoints and Composition,* Theatre Communications Group, 2004

Ben Brantley, Review of Richard Foreman's *Old-Fashioned Prostitutes* New York Times, May 7, 2013

Chapter 6

William Shakespeare, *As You Like It*

Robert J. Lifton, *The Protean Self,* Basic Books, 1993

Sonia Moore, *The Stanislavski System,* Penguin Handbooks, 1984

Ricky Gervais, *Extras* - season 2 episode 5

Chapter 7

Jean Paul Sartre, *Existentialism is a Humanism,* Lecture, 1946

Kenneth Burke, *Language as Symbolic Action,* University of California Press 1968

Patsy Rodenburg, *The Second Circle: How to Use*

Positive Energy for Success in Every Situation,
W. W. Norton & Company 2010

Chapter 8

Otto Rank, *Art and Artist: Creative Urge and Personality Development,* W. W. Norton & Company, 1989

Erving Goffman, *The Presentation of Self In Everyday Life* Anchor, 1959

Erikson, *Childhood and Society,* W. W. Norton & Company, 2013

Adrian M. S. Piper, Rationality and the Structure of the Self, Volume I: The Humean Conception andVolume II: A Kantian Conception (Berlin: APRA Foundation Berlin, 2013 (second edition)http://adrianpiper.com/rss/index.shtml). Chapter I."General Introduction to the Project: The Enterprise of Socratic Metaethics" (both volumes), page 10.

Chapter 9

García Lorca, *Theory and Play Of The Duende,* Translated by A. S. Kline © 2007

P. E. Easterling (Editor) *A Show for Dionysus The Cambridge Companion to Greek Tragedy,* Cambridge University Press, 1997.

http://www.psychologytoday.com/blog/thriving101/201001/what-science-has-say-about-genuine-vs-fake-smiles

Rodgers and Hammerstein, song: "You've Got to Be Taught" from South Pacific - 1949

Laura Marks, *Bethany*, Dramatists Play Service, 2013

Richard Schechner, *Grotowski Sourcebook* – Worlds of Performance, Routledge, 2001

Jean-Rene Toussaint Primitive Voice Workshop at the Wilma Theater (YouTube)

Patsy Rodenburg on YouTube: http://www.youtube.

com/watch?v=L9jjhGq8pMM

Edward Albee, *Who's Afraid of Virginia Woolf?,* Signet, 1983

Tennessee Williams, *A Streetcar Named Desire,* Signet, 1986

Kristin Linklater, *Freeing the Natural Voice,* Drama Publishers, 1976

Chapter 11

Arthur Miller, *Salesman in Bejing,* Viking Adult 1984

Arthur Miller, *Death of a Salesman,* Viking Press

Chapter 12

Henrik Ibsen, *Ibsen: Four Major Plays,* translated by Rick Davis and Brian Johnston, Smith & Kraus, 1995

Mabou Mines DollHouse video available on DVD.

Chapter 13

Anton Chekhov, *Ivanov,* translated by Carol Rocamora, Smith & Kraus, 1999

Anton Chekhov, *Chekhov: Four Plays,* translated by Carol Rocamora, Smith & Kraus, 1996

Chapter 14

William Shakespeare, *Hamlet*

Harold Bloom, *Hamlet: Poem Unlimited,* Riverhead Trade, 2004

Friedrich Nietzsche, *Birth of Tragedy and Genealogy of Morals* (Trans. Golffing), Doubleday / Anchor Books, 1956

Harold Bloom, The Modern Scholar: Shakespeare: The Seven Major Tragedies, Recorded Books, 2009

D.H. Lawrence, *Twilight in Italy,* Penguin Classics, 1997

IMAGES

70	Stanislavski Chart	Public Domain
74	Anton Chekhov	Public Domain
75	Vsevolod Meyerhold	Public Domain
76	Michael Chekhov	Public Domain
78	Stella Adler	Rue Faris Drew
77	Chekhov Class	Jeff Zinn
77	Chekhov Class	Jeff Zinn
77	Ronald Bennett	Jeff Zinn
78	Stella Adler	Rue Faris Drew
79	Harold Clurman	© Bettmann/Corbis
81	Lee Strasberg	Cynthia McAdams
81	Susan Batson	Susan Batson Studio
82	Julie Harris	Bob Tucker/Focalpoint Studio
84	Mesiner Class	Courtesy of The Neighborhood Playhouse photo archives
87	David Mamet	© Armando Gallo/Corbis
88	William H. Macy	© Greer Studios/Corbis
91	Susan Sontag	MDCarchives
93	Antonin Artaud	Public Domain
95	Bertolt Brecht	Public Domain
97	Jerzy Grotowski	Public Domain
99	Andre Gregory	© Cindy Kleine 2013
100	Robert Wilson	© Kaplanidis Yiorgos

155	Philip Seymour Hoffman	© Keith Bedford/ Reuters/ Corbis
158	Frederick Matthias Alexander	Public Domain
158	Kristin Linklater	Paula Langton
159	Jeff Zinn	Jeff Zinn
160	Zinn & Bennett	Jeff Zinn
161	Jean-René Toussaint	Jean-René Toussaint
162	*Trojan Women-*Andromache	Public Domain
172	*The Denial of Death* (cover)	Public Domain
179	Mabou Mines *Doll House*	Nancy Santos
184	*Hedda Gabler*	Jeff Zinn
193	*The Seagull*	Bob Tucker/Focalpoint studio
195	*Uncle Vanya*	Jeff Zinn
197	*Uncle Vanya*	Jeff Zinn
205	Harold Bloom	Michael Marsland, Yale
206	Sarah Bernhardt	Public Domain